THE AUGUSTAN REPRINT SOCIETY

A
VINDICATION
OF
PROVIDENCE:
OR, A
TRUE ESTIMATE
OF
Human LIFE.

(Second Edition, 1728)

EDWARD YOUNG

Introduction by
DAVID R. ANDERSON

Publication Numbers 225–226
WILLIAM ANDREWS CLARK MEMORIAL LIBRARY
University of California, Los Angeles
1984

109630

GENERAL EDITOR
> DAVID STUART RODES, *University of California, Los Angeles*

EDITORS
> CHARLES L. BATTEN, *University of California, Los Angeles*
> GEORGE ROBERT GUFFEY, *University of California, Los Angeles*
> MAXIMILLIAN E. NOVAK, *University of California, Los Angeles*
> NANCY MALIM SHEA, *William Andrews Clark Memorial Library*
> THOMAS WRIGHT, *William Andrews Clark Memorial Library*

ADVISORY EDITORS
> PAULA R. BACKSCHEIDER, *University of Rochester*
> RALPH COHEN, *University of Virginia*
> WILLIAM E. CONWAY, *William Andrews Clark Memorial Library*
> VINTON A. DEARING, *University of California, Los Angeles*
> PHILLIP HARTH, *University of Wisconsin, Madison*
> ROBERT D. HUME, *Pennsylvania State University*
> MRS. DONALD F. HYDE, *Somerville, New Jersey*
> LOUIS A. LANDA, *Princeton University*
> EARL MINER, *Princeton University*
> JAMES SUTHERLAND, *University College, London*
> NORMAN J. W. THROWER, *William Andrews Clark Memorial Library*
> ROBERT VOSPER, *William Andrews Clark Memorial Library*
> JOHN M. WALLACE, *University of Chicago*

PUBLICATIONS MANAGER
> NANCY MALIM SHEA, *William Andrews Clark Memorial Library*

CORRESPONDING SECRETARY
> BEVERLY J. ONLEY, *William Andrews Clark Memorial Library*

Introduction ©1984 by The William Andrews Clark Memorial Library
University of California, Los Angeles
2520 Cimarron Street, Los Angeles, California 90018

Designed and printed by The Castle Press, Pasadena, California

INTRODUCTION

THE SUDDEN DEATH of George I while on a visit to his native Hanover in June 1727 diverted the attention of England's politicians and poets who looked for or depended upon royal favor toward the Prince of Wales, now George II, and his consort, Caroline.[1] Among the place holders affected by the succession was Edward Young, then forty-three years old, the chaplain to Caroline and the author of various occasional poems, three tragedies, five popular verse satires, and a body of religious poetry which included a paraphrase of the book of Job.[2] At the time of the king's death Young, who had not yet been given a living in the Church, was busy lobbying Lord Carteret, Lord Lieutenant of Ireland, for preferment.[3] He must have seen, however, that a sermon on this occasion, in addition to demonstrating why he should be continued as Caroline's chaplain, would provide the perfect opportunity to demonstrate his fitness for further royal preferment in the Church. Accordingly, he responded with one of his most famous sermons, *A Vindication of Providence: Or, A True Estimate of Human Life*, which he preached before George II and Caroline "in St. *George's* Church near *Hanover-Square*, soon after the late *King's* Death."[4]

Despite its significance for his future, Young may not have written the piece specifically for this occasion. If his letter to Thomas Tickell on 24 October 1724 referring to "a Piece of Divinity wh[ich] I have finished by me" does indeed, as one editor suggests, allude to the *True Estimate*, he simply adapted and preached a sermon already at hand.[5] In any case, the work was a success and quickly found its way into print with a dedication to the queen.[6] The published version was, however, almost certainly expanded from the actual sermon Young delivered: "It is impossible to believe," as one writer says, "without feeling intense sympathy for his hearers, that he delivered from St. George's pulpit the whole of the discourse as it was published. . . ."[7]

Young lost no time in using the published version of his sermon to bolster his claims for preferment. Doubtless he hoped that the dedication to Queen Caroline, "One of the Principal *Ornaments* of Human Life" (sig. A3r), would promote his chances for royal preferment, but he also used the piece to buttress his suit to Lord Carteret and others. He sent a copy to Tickell on 17 November 1727 with this note: "For want of others writings to amuse you with, I have sent you a sermon, wh[ich] I desire you to accept, & to convey a Copy to Mr Clutterbuck, & my Ld Carteret with my Duty." Three months later he sent another copy, fearing that the first had "miscarryd" in the mail, and two months after that he enclosed a copy of the second edition, which Tickell was to give to Carteret only "if you think such a present may do more good than harm." Young also alludes to the *True Estimate* in his letter to the king's mistress, Henrietta Howard, afterwards Countess of Suffolk, which begs her efforts on his behalf, in part on the grounds that "I have Written nothing, without showing my Duty to their Majestys, & some Pieces are Dedicated to Them."[8]

But Young's ambitions for this piece did not rest even there. He intended it to form the first half of a two-part prose theodicy based on Colossians 3:2—"*Set your Affections on Things above, and not on Things on the Earth.*" The second half, however, never appeared, nor did Young ever seem disposed to supply it. In November 1746, shortly before *A True Estimate* was reprinted by Samuel Richardson for Henry Lintot (imprint date 1747), Young wrote in a letter to Richardson, "Pray my service to Mr. Lintot. I thought of making some additions to that piece; but, on second thoughts, I let it alone; so that it may go to the press as it is." Sixteen years later, in a letter to a Mrs. Anne Brett, Young claimed, "The second part of the thing you speak of, I wrote at Lyons in France; where, by the carelessness of a servant, it was left behind, nor could I ever recover it."[9]

Even without the second half, it is possible to infer from *A True Estimate* the overall shape of Young's argument as conceived, though not fully executed. Young's text from Colossians distinguishes sharply between the "Things on the Earth" and the "Things above"; accordingly, the two-part discourse was to reinforce that distinction by weighing earthly things in the balance against those of Heaven. The first half of Young's argument, the *True Estimate*, describes "the *General* State of Mankind" (95), while the second half was to show how that grim state could be ameliorated by proper attention to the things of Heaven. This projected bipartite structure, based on the scriptural passage, explains why the treatise we have reads less like a vindication of the ways of God to man than an essay on the vanity of human wishes: Young never supplied the counterbalancing vision of heavenly things.

The theodicy of the projected two-part discourse intersects with its Pauline contempt of earthly things. In his dedication, Young offers *A True Estimate* to the queen as a vindication of Providence from the charge that humans must necessarily be unhappy on earth. Without absolutely denying the reality of evil, he argues that if the things on the earth are insufficient to our peace, the fault is not God's but ours for misusing and misprizing them. We need not be as miserable as the published half of the argument finds us. Presumably, its second half would have developed this argument in detail; as it is, Young offers only the assertion that Providence enables us to be happier than we choose to be.

Without forgetting its larger context, one can still read *A True Estimate* as a self-contained essay. Its organization, though complex, clearly reflects its thematic unity. After a brief introduction emphasizing the necessity for a Christian to work out his own salvation "notwithstanding all our Lord has done to save us" (1) and a brief exegesis of the text—Young calls it "explaining the Words" (3)—the sermon moves into its most important stage: explaining how to perform the injunction of the text. We are to think of, to judge, and to love the things above. Young quickly disposes of the topic of thinking of things above in order to dwell on judging them by comparing them with things of the earth. The third part of our duty, loving the things above, he reserves for the second, unpublished, half of his argument.

Young divides the "Things on the Earth" into the *Orders, Ages, Aims, Relations, Constitutions, Tempers,* and *Passions* of Men" (11), disposing of the first five topics quickly. Riches, for example, produce high expectations which in turn produce high resentment when they are unfulfilled; youth desires more than age and is thus more easily disappointed; those who aim high suffer disappointment while those who aim low fear for the loss of what they have attained; tender relations make us fear death while painful ones poison our peace; a healthy constitution brings temptation and a sickly one pain. The tempers, which Young regards as "lesser *Passions*" (30), occupy a sort of no-man's-land between his fifth and his final topics; they, too, "have all their peculiar Evils" (30).

All of this takes Young roughly one-third of the way through his discourse, the rest of which he devotes to an essay on the passions—except for two concluding sections, one which explains what all of this has to do with the death of the king and another which offers a compelling summary of the insufficiency of the "Things on the Earth." The prominence accorded Young's analysis of the passions, both by his subtitle—"in which the *Passions* are consider'd in a New Light"—and by the amount of space he devotes to it—more than half the discourse—testifies to its importance in his eyes. Young's great interest in the passions doubtless stems from the crucial role he assigned to them in the process by which our affections fasten on either things above or things on the earth. Because they are "the Wants of the Soul, as the Appetites may be call'd the Passions of the Body" (49), they "give the *perpetual Motion* to Human Life" and "roll us from Place to Place, from Object to Object" (34). Love, for example, if not properly directed, becomes mere voluptuousness, ambition, avarice, or vanity—all of which set their affections on the things of the earth; properly channeled, however, love seeks the things of Heaven. Thus, an understanding of and ability to control the passions are essential to obeying the scriptural injunction which serves as Young's text.

In analyzing the way the passions deflect our affections from the things of Heaven, Young pays particular attention to ambition, a subject he had already taken up in another work—*Love of Fame: The Universal Passion* (1725-28). These verse satires mainly attack the ridiculous effects of ambition, but in the final half of satire 7 (published in 1728) Young turns to an explanation of the cause of man's inordinate love of fame. Originally, that passion came as the gift of Heaven, "To warm, to raise, to deify, mankind."[10] Because of the love of fame by "large-soul'd men" (*Works*, 2:137), laws, the arts, and patriotism all arose. In modern days, however, that mission has been distorted:

> But, oh! this passion planted in the soul,
> On eagle's wings to mount her to the pole,
> The flaming minister of virtue meant,
> Set up false gods, and wrong'd her high descent.
> (*Works,* 2:137)

When linked with virtue, ambition prospers; when it works alone, it becomes the object of the preacher's anger and the satirist's lash.

A True Estimate sees the dangers of ambition as much more absolute. Young does not reflect in his sermon upon the benefits of ambition; on the contrary, he argues that even the good passions bring with them "Inconveniences, and Inquietudes" (45). The benefits of ambition might have found their place in the projected second half of Young's argument. In his sermon, the portrait of them is a dark one. In the satires Young adopts a poetical persona and in the sermon a clerical one. This, too, accounts for the difference in treatment: the preacher of *A True Estimate* finds very little to laugh at in overaffection for ambition; it is not folly but iniquity.

Young's biblical text for his sermon could have served equally well as the epigraph for his greatest poem, *The Complaint, Or Night-Thoughts on Life, Death, and Immortality* (1742-45). Both open with a frank acknowledgment of death, but the sermon, preached on the death of a king, teaches a lesson sadly needed by the poem's speaker, who is wrapped in impious grief over the death of three loved ones. In fact, the speaker of *Night Thoughts* plainly commits the sin of setting his affections on the things of the earth, not on things above. He maintains a false estimate of human life until he convinces himself that man is immortal. Similarly, Lorenzo, the chameleonlike adversary—now a skeptic, now a materialist, now a man of pleasure—must set his affections on the things above, a change of heart which it becomes the speaker's task to promote. The speaker becomes, in effect, the preacher: "What, if for once," he asks Lorenzo, "I preach thee quite awake?" (*Works,* 1:17).

The *Night Thoughts* ranges broadly through the inner and outer worlds while *A True Estimate*, with its emphasis on the passions, takes in a much more modest scope. Nevertheless, the sermon offers much the same argument on those points where they intersect. Night 8, "Virtue's Apology," for example, answers the man of the world by pointing out how "the world," ambition, and pleasure constitute triple bolts that kill virtue. Ambition, the speaker reminds Lorenzo, counts for nought; it only produces discomfort to those who suffer its goad. In seeking the applause of the many, Lorenzo becomes their slave: "Denied the public eye, the public voice, / As if he liv'd on others' breath, he dies" (*Works*, 1:197). These are the points made in *A True Estimate* as well, where the ambitious man, "all Expectation" (69), is a slave to the multitude. But the *Night Thoughts* goes beyond the attack on ambition and other sinful passions to offer the consolation that a humble heart will win the love of God and eternal life. *A True Estimate* focuses on the things on the earth; once again, its picture is grimmer. Nevertheless, it sees in the death of the king a cure for ambition. A providential warning, the king's death reminds the worldly man of his worldly fate and turns "his Affections into their right Channel" and sends them "forward to their proper End" (78).

A True Estimate is clearly important for students of Young, but it also deserves to be better known generally among readers of eighteenth-century literature. The art of moral discipline concerned other writers than Young, most notably the Samuel Johnson of the *Rambler* essays, and even though Young cannot approach Johnson's sympathy for the human condition or his moral gravity, *A True Estimate* demonstrates again how deeply aware the century was of the power and potential treachery of the passions. For Young, "a Mind haunted with Fear is a hideous Night-Piece of Storm, Precipice, Ruins, Tombs, and Apparitions" (38); elsewhere, he observes of the passions that they "*pain* the whole Soul, they *confound* the Memory, *make wild* the Imagination, and *hurt* the Understanding" (49); and he offers a Johnsonian perspective on the passions of an ambitious man which leave him "never at Home to the present Hour, but reaching, and gasping [sic] at Joys to come" (55). Young and Johnson both ask the question, "Where then shall Hope and Fear their objects find?" (*The Vanity of Human Wishes*, line 343). Johnson answers with prayer that leaves to Heaven the measure and the choice; Young answers with Colossians 3:2. Young's answer may not seem as hard-won as Johnson's, but the reader of *A True Estimate* will concede that he poses the question memorably.

If the passions bedevil us and mortality plagues us, what is human happiness? The concluding sixteen pages of *A True Estimate* draw back from the close analysis of the passions occupying much of the work to ask that question. Even remembering that Young intended to balance this concluding portrait of human life with a treatise on the things of Heaven, it is difficult to reconcile the sustained and eloquent pessimism of this concluding section with the claim of Young's dedication that he will vindicate Providence from the charge of creating a world where humans are bound to misery. Not even Johnson's world, where "Infelicity is involved in corporeal nature, and interwoven with our being" (*Rambler* 32), seems more bleak. Young finally paints a world where "we are Born with Pain, and Die with Amazement," one struggling under the Virgilian rubric, "*Sunt Lacrymae Rerum, & mentem Mortalia tangunt*" (92). In the absence of the second half of *A True Estimate*, we cannot help being moved by this desolate portrait of human life. We may look to *Night Thoughts* for a response to this bleak picture, but even then the sermon's force remains. Young, the poet of the graveyard and of the glorious dawn of resurrection, appears in *A True Estimate* as an equally effective chronicler of the vanity of human wishes.

Texas A & M University
College Station

NOTES TO THE INTRODUCTION

1. On the interesting circumstances surrounding the death of George I, see Ragnhild Hatton, *George I: Elector and King* (Cambridge, Mass.: Harvard University Press, 1978), 280-85. Lord Hervey's memoirs chronicle some of the place scrambling that followed the king's death. See *Some Materials Towards Memoirs of the Reign of King George II. By John, Lord Hervey*, ed. Romney Sedgwick, 3 vols. (1931; reprint, New York: AMS Press, 1970), 1:22-49.

2. In addition to his post as Caroline's chaplain, Young had been awarded a pension in 1726 of £200 per annum by George I. See *The Correspondence of Edward Young, 1683-1765*, ed. Henry Pettit (Oxford: Clarendon Press, 1971), 47 n. 2. Both pension and royal post were held at the king's pleasure.

3. Young applied to Carteret because as Lord Lieutenant of Ireland he would have many livings to fill there. See Isabel St. John Bliss, *Edward Young*, Twayne's English Authors Series, 80 (New York: Twayne Publishers, 1969), 74. The classic attack on Young's place seeking is George Eliot's brilliant "Worldliness and Other-Worldliness: The Poet Young" (1857), in *Essays of George Eliot*, ed. Thomas Pinney (New York: Columbia University Press, 1963), 335-85. Bliss offers a more sympathetic view in chapter 4.

4. I quote from the title page as reproduced below. The sermon, incidentally, did no more for its author than the siege of Carteret. Young finally received a living in 1730 from All Souls, Oxford.

5. Pettit's guess (34 n. 2) seems plausible to me, especially since *A True Estimate* is not organized on the topic of the king's death. That subject comes in rather awkwardly near the end (77-79) and could well have been added to an already existing piece. On the other hand, Young explicitly writes that the death of the king "first suggested *This Subject* to me" (77). Throughout the later eighteenth century and the nineteenth, this piece was commonly known by its short title, *A True Estimate*, which I adopt here.

6. The *Monthly Chronicle* for November 1727 announces that the sermon has just been published; the same journal announced the publication of a second edition in January 1727/8. See Pettit, 58 n. 4 and 62 n. 2. A third edition appeared in 1729, a fourth in 1729, and a fifth in 1737.

7. Henry C. Shelley, *The Life and Letters of Edward Young* (1914; reprint, St. Clair Shores, Mich.: Scholarly Press, 1970), 95. Young himself felt it necessary to account for the length of the published version. His preface declares, "I hope the Great *Length* will be excused, since the Na-

ture of the Subject might easily have betray'd me into a much greater Transgression against the Common Limits of This kind of Writing" (sig. A4v; italics reversed).

8. For these letters see Pettit as follows: Young to Thomas Tickell on 17 November 1727, 58–59; 5 February 1727/8, 60–62; and 14 April 1728, 65; and Young to Henrietta Howard, [?April–May 1730], 67–69. Pettit assumes that the piece referred to in these letters is in fact *A True Estimate* even though sometimes the evidence for this assumption is largely circumstantial. I believe his assumption is correct.

9. For these two letters see Pettit as follows: Young to Samuel Richardson on 11 November 1746, 246–48; and Young to Anne Brett, [?September 1762], 562. Again, in the case of the last letter we must assume that the work referred to is *A True Estimate*. In the "Life of Young" by Herbert Croft in Johnson's *Lives of the Poets*, we find a less plausible but more interesting suggestion as to the fate of the second half: "What he calls 'The *true* estimate of Human Life' . . . exhibits only the wrong side of the tapestry; and being asked why he did not show the right, he is said to have replied he could not; though by others it has been told me that this was finished, but that a lady's monkey tore it in pieces before there existed any copy." See Samuel Johnson, *Lives of the English Poets*, ed. George Birkbeck Hill, 3 vols. (1905; reprint, New York: Octagon Books, 1967), 3:378–79.

10. *The Poetical Works of Edward Young*, 2 vols., The Aldine Edition of the British Poets (n.d.; reprint, Westport, Conn.: Greenwood Press, 1970), 2:137. All quotations from Young's other works are from this edition, subsequently cited in the text as *Works*; references are to volume and page (this edition lacks line numbers).

BIBLIOGRAPHICAL NOTE

A Vindication of Providence: Or, A True Estimate of Human Life (1728) is reproduced from the copy of the "SECOND EDITION Corrected" in the Clark Library (Shelf Mark: *PR3782/V71/1728). A typical type page (7) measures 166 x 85 mm.

A VINDICATION OF PROVIDENCE:

OR, A TRUE ESTIMATE OF Human LIFE.

IN WHICH THE
Paſſions are conſider'd in a New Light.

Preach'd in St. *George*'s Church near *Hanover Square*, ſoon after the late *King*'s Death.

The SECOND EDITION Corrected.

By E. YOUNG, LL. D. Fellow of *All Souls* College in *Oxford*.

LONDON:
Printed for T. WORRALL, at the *Judge*'s Head over againſt St. *Dunſtan*'s Church in *Fleet-ſtreet*. 1728.

TO THE
QUEEN.

MADAM,

F the following Discourse is as Happy in its Execution, as it is Important in its Design, It will not be, (give me leave to say,) altogether unworthy of a Royal Patronage.

THE Design is of great Consequence; and, I think, New: It is to remove a Prevailing, and Inveterate Mistake, which first sprang, and now thrives in a Soil too indulgent to it, and a soil too difficultly subdu'd, the *Pride*, and *Ill-Nature*, and *Melancholy*, and *Vice* of mankind. I mean, MADAM, That false Opinion, that Refle-

DEDICATION.

&ction on Providence, " That This World
" is, in its own Nature, That is, by God's
" Appointment, a World of Sorrow, a
" Scene of Misery, a Vale of Tears; and
" that to *Be* in it, is to *Be wretched* un-
" avoidably." Whereas this Treatise shall endeavour to make it manifest, That Providence is not only Gracious in the Composition, Studious of the Accommodation, Preventive of the Accidents, Corrective of the Mistakes, and Liberal to the Wants, but Lavish, also, to the Luxuries of Man; and that God does not only permit, but *enable* us, and not only enable, but *enjoyn* us, to be Happy; Happy, to a much greater Degree than we are, That is, than we *chuse* to be.

NOR is that Error I combat, an Error of the Vulgar, Unlearned, or Sinful only; But the Learned, Wise, and Good, have fatally contributed their sacred Authority towards the Propagation, and Establishment of it: Either through Inadvertency, or the Resentment of *present* Pain, or an indiscreet, tho' well-intended Zeal, in the recommendation of a Better World.

MOST

DEDICATION.

MOST of them have, as it were casually, let fall from their Pens, which pursu'd some other Principal Point, too severe, and unguarded Intimations to the Discredit of our *present* State: *Many* have made an Invective on this Life, a *general* Drift that mingled itself in all their Discourses, and Conversations: And *some* have made it their *particular* Theme, and avowdly, determinately, and strictly drove at this very Point; without adjoyning the true Causes, the proper Cures, the right Uses, and salutary Effects of *our* Misfortunes and Pains; and thus have left *Grounds*, of Future Argument against the *Goodness*, and thrown a Present Cloud over the *Glory* of the Great Disposer of Events, the *King* of *Time*, and of *Eternity*.

LET, MADAM, One of his most shining Representatives on Earth, patronize, and vindicate a *Vindication* of *His Providence*; Let One of the Principal *Ornaments of Human Life* indulge *a True Estimate of it*; Let Her graciously defend a Refutation of an Error, which flows from a Decay of That *Faith*, of which our dread Sovereign

DEDICATION.

Sovereign is the Great *Defender*; and, which leads to a Corruption of That *Morality*, of which her own correct Conduct is the Distinguish'd *Glory*. Let that Queen who is nearly concern'd in the *sad Occasion* that turn'd my Thought on this Subject, take it into Her Protection; Her *Protection* will recommend it to the World, and Her *Example* will supply the Defects of this Composition on it.

AND, Madam, as your Example *will* assist me, So that Good Providence, whose Ways I presume to assert, Grant, that Your Fortune *may* too! That Your most sacred Majesty, from this joyful, and unclouded *Morning* of your Reign, may shine forth a long, and illustrious *Day*, as an unanswerable *Instance* of *Temporal* Happiness, and an unquestionable *Heir* of *Eternal*, is the constant, and fervent Prayer of

MADAM,

Your Majesty's most Obedient,

And most Dutiful Subject

E. YOUNG.

The PREFACE.

 KNOW not well why, but the Passions are a Favourite Subject with Mankind: The Reason may possibly be, Because Men are much concern'd with them, both as to themselves, and Others; and where we have a Self-concern, we have an Attention. Or, Because they are such Powerful, and Universal Springs, that almost all the Pleasures, Pains, Designs, and Actions of Life are owing to Them; and therefore it is our Interest to know them well: Or, Because every Man carrying them in his own Breast, He thinks he knows them well already, and is therefore an Able Judge of such Compositions; And thus his Pride has a Fondness for them: Or, Because the Passions, like the Boy at the Fountain, fall in love with their own Representation: Or, Because many are all Passion, and if Men consider a Treatise on the Passions, as a History of Themselves, it is no wonder they read it with Pleasure. Or, Because what a most celebrated Antient writ on this Subject is lost, to the great Regret of the Learned, and Polite World, which is studious of some Reparation of that Loss; and the more so, because what other Antients have left on that Head, is Imperfect, and Short.

BEING sensible how difficult it is to gain Attention for Works of Divinity, I have insisted more on the Passions, than any other Head of the following Discourse; in hopes of a more welcome Reception prepar'd for it, by that general Tast, or Disposition of Heart, which I have mentioned. I have mark'd the Distinctions, and Peculiarities of the Passions, with some Care.

A French Author, has treated of them with such Accuracy, and Applause, that it conciliated to him the particular Favour of a Celebrated Queen, who wept for the Death of the Author of that Piece, though she had never seen the Man.

BUT

The PREFACE.

BUT He had a wrong *Byass* on him through the Whole *to the Prejudice of it*; Nor could I reap any Advantage from Him beside that of having such an Example of *Industry*, and *Discernment*; of which, what *Use* I have made I do not Hope, but Fear the Reader will too easily perceive. That Author indeed displays the *Passions* at large, and pursues them into all their several *Branches*, whereas I could find Room for the *Primary*, or *Radical Passions* only, at present; but they may, one Day shoot, under Her Majesty's benign *Influence*, (who like the *Queen* above-mentioned, is the greatest Encourager of *Arts*) and give that one *Tree* of *Human Knowledge* its entire Growth.

BUT as Imperfect as the Discourse now is, (of which I am very sensible) I persuade my self the Reader will find an Uncommon *Variety* in it; And that the Observations, which are by no Means drawn from *Books*, but the *Life*, are so far Just, That any one who is at the Pains of looking on them, may possibly find *Truths* which his own Experience can attest, and thus be a Witness, as well as a Judge of what is Here written: He may find some *Traces*, some Features of his own Condition, as the Trojon met his own Picture on a Foreign Shore. I wish, (a rare Wish in a Writer) that I could be refuted in what is Here advanc'd, for some of the Truths are very melancholy. I hope the Great *Length* will be excused, since the Nature of the *Subject* might easily have betray'd me into a much greater *Transgression* against the Common Limits of *This* kind of *Writing*.

IF this Piece in any tollerable Degree answer its *Title*, a Perusal will not be thrown away upon it. For I look on it as one of the Desiderata in Literature, and that of the nearest, and most General Concern to Man.

The Second Discourse will be Publish'd soon.

COLOSS. iii. 2.

Set your Affections on Things above, and not on Things on the Earth.

E by no Means question, but that the Birth, and Life, and Death, and Resurrection of our Lord, were Acts of infinite Merit; Merit sufficient to satisfy God's Justice, and bring Sinners to the Terms of Reconcilement, and Salvation: But we must not imagine that they wrought any Change, or Confusion in the Nature of Things. God is as pure as ever, and Iniquity is as much his Aversion: Tho' he can be reconciled to *Sinners*, he cannot be reconciled to *Sin*; and tho' the Sinner may be saved, he cannot be *saved* unless he, first, be *changed*; for Heaven has no more Admittance for Corruption, than it had before. And therefore the unchangeable Holiness of God requires, that, notwithstanding all our Lord has done to save us, we should still *work out our own Salva-*

Salvation, by a Conformity to his *Example*, as well as a Dependance on his *Merit*; nor, moſt impiouſly, make his Merit an Encouragement of Sin.

FOR this Reaſon, the Chriſtian is called on to be born, to live, to die, and to riſe again, in a *Moral* Senſe; for in the *Natural*, all theſe Acts are Acts of Neceſſity. Theſe Expreſſions import ſo many ſeveral Stages in the Chriſtian Courſe.

BY *Nature* we are born of Fleſh and Blood, which gives us a Conſtitution fond of what is *preſent*, and careleſs of what is *future:* And therefore to ſecure the future, we are told, that the Spirit of God is a new Principle of Life, which, when received into the Soul, will impreſs on it new Thoughts, new Aims, and new Deſires; and to receive this Principle, and theſe Impreſſions, is the Chriſtian *Birth*.

BY *Nature* we live a Life of Senſe and Self-will, which is deſtructive of our eternal Intereſt; and therefore we are enjoined to take the Will of Chriſt for our Rule, and his Practice for our Example; and this is the Chriſtian *Life*.

BY *Nature* we die thro' a Separation of Soul and Body; but this Separation makes it well with none, with whom it was not well before; and therefore we are enjoined to die to Sin; and this is the Chriſtian *Death*.

BY *Nature* (or by God's Appointment in Nature) we are to rise again, whether we will, or no; but nothing that is of pure Force can produce an Effect to any one's spiritual Advantage; and therefore are we to rise by Choice, that is, *by setting our Affections on Things above*; and this is the Christian *Resurrection*; the Perfection of the Christian State, and that which the Text particularly calls for.

I SHALL begin with explaining the Words. The first Word in the original Text contains the whole Act of our Duty: We translate it, *set your Affections*; but more is implyed in it. We cannot *love* any Thing without *judging* of its Worth; or can we *judge* of the Worth of any Thing, without taking it into our *Thoughts*; and the Word signifies each of these Acts, to * *think*, to † *judge*, and to § *love*. Thus the whole Signification of the Word not only teaches us the whole *Act* of our Duty, but likewise the *Method* necessary for the Practice of it; *think*, *judge*, and then *love*.

THE next Words are *Things above*: Shewing the Object of our Duty. Now Things above, in the Style of Scripture, signifies the Things of *Grace*, and the Things of *Glory*. The Things of *Grace*, are Holiness, Justice, Temperance, Charity, and all other Christian

---
* Rom. 12.   † Rom. 14. 6.   § In the Text.

Vertues,

Virtues. Prov. xv. 24. *The Way of Life is above to the Wife, that he may depart from Hell beneath;* that is, every wife Man will be religious; for this is the Way above, that upper, exalted Way that leads to Life: But Sin is the low, and ignominious Way; so low, that there is nothing beneath it but Hell, to which it leads.

SECONDLY, by Things above, are meant the Things of *Glory;* as the beatifick Vision of God, the Presence of Christ, the Conversation of Angels, the Fellowship of Saints; Bodies glorified, Souls ennobled, Faculties enlarged, and entertained with transporting Objects, and replenished with unmixed Joys! All these Things are meant by Things above: And one would imagine that an Injunction could not be ungrateful, to *set our Affections* on Things like these.

AND yet it is ungrateful to most of us; and that for this Reason, because there are Things on the Earth too, Things contrary in their *Nature,* and inconsistent in their *Choice,* with the Things now mentioned: Pleasant Things, and such whose Pleasures are present, and palpable, and always at hand: Pleasures of Appetite and Sense, those winning Masters, under whose Dominion we spend the first of our Years for *want* of Reason, and (too often) the rest, in *spite* of it: Pleasures, that thro' their Number, and Opportunity, and Prepossession, and Custom, get such a fatal Ascendant,

cendant, that unless we are always on our Guard against them, our Love of *Things above* will either never spring, or (what is all one) never come to Maturity. And this is the Reason of that Caution superadded in the last Words of the Text, *not on Things on the Earth.*

HAVING thus explained the Words, I proceed to shew the particular Method of practising the Duty contained in them; which consists (as I have already intimated) in those three Acts; First, Thinking of; Secondly, Judging; Thirdly, Loving the *Things above.*

TO *think* of them is the Beginning of our Duty. Nothing can act on the Soul but by the Mediation of Thought; that which we think not of, moves us no more than that which is not: And therefore it is not so much the Beauty, or Excellency, or Gratefulness, or Fitness of an Object, as Thought that makes us love. The Object brings in the Matter, but Thought gives the Form to the Passion; and if we think not of a Thing, it is impossible we should love it, be it never so lovely.

IF therefore we would work our selves to a proper Zeal for *Things above*, it is necessary that we should allow our selves stated Seasons of thinking on them: We must call them into our Mind, and make them the Matter of our serious Contemplation, and then the most desirable Things will certainly move in us a suitable Desire. NOR

NOR is it strange that Thought should be necessary to give us an *Affection* for Things *Spiritual* and *remote*, when it is necessary to give us a *Perception* of Things *sensible*, and *at hand*. The Eye may be open on an Object which it does not see; and the Ear struck with Sounds which it does not hear, if Thought is intensely engag'd another Way. But small Attention, indeed, is necessary to give Things sensible, and present their full Force on us. And this is the Reason of that Advantage which earthly Things have on our Choice, above heavenly: They are Immediate; their *Presence* is their *Power*. But religious *Thought*, and that only, can rob them of this fatal Advantage; which is a strong Argument for the Practice of this Duty: Thought can make absent Things present, take away the Distance between Earth and Heaven, and make an eternal Good, though future, a better Entertainment, and fuller Satisfaction to the Mind, than all the Pleasures of Sin, tho' at hand.

I CONFESS, indeed, since Heaven forces it self on our Thoughts, from a thousand Occasions, whether we will, or no; that many think of Heaven, and yet do not desire it as much as they ought; but this I affirm, that every Man desires it in Proportion to his Thinking: For no Man but wishes for Heaven, while Heaven is on his Mind; and if every transient Glance of Thought can procure

A True Estimate of Human Life. 7

procure a *Wish*, it is a good Argument, that a fixed, and frequent Contemplation would produce no less than an effectual *Will*. If therefore we affect not Heaven enough, it is because we contemplate it too little.

INDEED there is one strange Consideration which offers it self on this Subject: Since our common Notion of Things above represents them as infinitely preferable to all other, how is it possible that they should not ever engage our Thoughts? how is it possible, that Mankind which abhors nothing so much as Pain, should not be for ever meditating on that Place, which we confess to be the Seat of perfect Exemption from it? how is it possible, that Mankind which toils out a weary Life in eager Pursuits of every *Appearance of Good*, should forget That which we confess the *Supream?* For it is too manifest, that as the Thoughts of Heaven, and heavenly Things enter most *rarely* into our Minds, so they hang the most *loosely* there, and are soonest dislodged from their slender Hold on us. Every new Object, tho' never so trifling, foreign, or absurd, is sufficient to divert us from the Importance of them.

THE Holy Scripture is frequent in asserting, that the Devil is actually, and perpetually conversant among us. His End and Business being to seduce, deceive, and destroy. Nor can there be a greater human Demonstration of this Truth, than this Instance of our Thoughts, with regard to the Contemplation of eternal Happiness; wherein their Slackness, Avocations, Startings, Wanderings, and Interruptions, are so unaccountable, so contrary to their Nature and Manner of Attention, when applied to worldly Objects, that they cannot seem to receive their Conduct from any Principle, either Voluntary, or Mechanical, that is purely within our selves, but from the extrinsick Influence, and Injection of that evil Spirit. And accordingly we find him charged, *Mat.* xiii. 19. with this very Fact of snatching away *Good Thoughts* from the Heart of Man.

AND, indeed, if Men but grant that there is such a Power, and that he can tempt us, (which, if we deny, we must cease to be Christians,) the Other follows of it self: For the *Region* of the Soul, in which the Devil forges his Wiles to deceive us, is the *Imagination*; and his *Manner* of working is by forming Images, or exciting Motions there, which become the immediate Matter of our Thought; and his *Time* of working is then particularly, when he perceives our Minds are religiously disposed; for then he is most afraid of losing his Hold on us. And thence comes to pass (what I fear all of us have perceived) that at the Seasons of Devotion a Languor, and Inattention often comes over us, which we feel neither before, nor after: For then especially,

he

he attempts our Imagination, and throngs it with foreign Matter. As therefore my Text requires the *setting our Thoughts on Things above*, in Order to create such a Relish, and kindle such a Desire as is due to them; so, in order to setting our Thoughts on them, it is necessary to superadd this Rule; That in the Seasons assigned for such Contemplation, we should always guard our Thoughts with that Petition in the Lord's Prayer, *Deliver us from Evil*, that Evil-one (as it may be rendered) who is ever hovering round us to snatch away good Thoughts from our Hearts.

BUT a Persuasive to serious Contemplation (and nothing less than serious Contemplation is sufficient) must seem strange to so gay an Age, which has distinguished it self by nothing more, than by carrying Diversions to their greatest, and most expensive Height; *Diversions*, which are the Reverse of serious *Thought*: An Age, which particularly may be said with *Sempronia*, * Psallere, & saltare elegantius quam necesse est Probæ. Pecuniæ, an* Famæ *minus parceret haud facile discerneres*. I cannot therefore but repeat what cannot, I think, fail of some Effect on all that hear it attentively.

"AH, my Friends! while we *laugh*, all
"Things are *serious* round about us: God is
"serious, who exerciseth Patience toward us;

---
* Salust.

"Chrift is ferious, who fhed his Blood for us; the Holy Ghoft is ferious, who ftriveth a- gainft the Obftinacy of our Hearts; the Holy Scriptures bring to our Ears the moft ferious Things in the World; the Holy Sacraments reprefent the moft ferious, and awful Matters; the whole Creation is ferious in ferving God, and us; all that are in Heaven, or Hell, are ferious; how, then, can we be gay?" To give thefe excellent Words their full Force, it fhould be known, that they came not from the *Priefthood*, but the *Court*; and from a Courtier as eminent as *England* ever boafted.

I SHALL now proceed to my *fecond* Head, *Judging* of the *Things above*; which is the fecond Act of our Duty. As *judging* of them without *thinking*, which fome do, (or our Converfations and Preffes would not be fo guilty as they are,) is prepofterous; fo *thinking* of them without *judging*, is incom- petent, and fhort. We muft therefore *judge* likewife of the *Things above*; that is, we muft *think* of them *comparatively*, weigh them a- gainft all other Things, that may poffibly ftand in Competition with them; and fo on a rational, and mature Deliberation, give them that Preference which they fo well deferve.

NOW this *fecond* Act of the Soul is ne- ceffary for the fixing our Affections, for *this* Reafon; becaufe the fimple Act of *Thinking*, indifferently raifes our Love to every Thing
that

A true Estimate of Human Life.

that is pleasurable; but when *Judgment* comes to examine, and discern between those pleasurable Things, it will find that some of them must be foregone, and rejected of Necessity, because they are inconsistent *with*, and destructive *of* each other. And this, in a particular Manner, is the Case between *Things above*, *and Things upon the Earth*; both of them offer Pleasures, and such Pleasures as must necessarily engage our Affections, on our first Contemplation of them: But those two Kinds of Pleasures are inconsistent; so contrary to each other, both in their Nature, and their Means, that it is impossible for *one* Soul to pursue both; such, therefore, as entertain a distracted Inclination for both of them, are called in Scripture, Men of *two* Souls.

SINCE, then, it is necessary to *chuse* one, in Order to enjoy *either*, let our *Judgment* examine these two Competitors for our Affections, *Things above*, and *Things upon the Earth*, and see which of them is most likely to bring in the fullest Satisfaction to our Souls.

FIRST, let us put this World in the Ballance; and to avoid Confusion in so wide a Subject, let us separately consider the different *Orders*, *Ages*, *Aims*, *Relations*, *Constitutions*, *Tempers*, and *Passions* of Men; and see this *Variety united* in Uneasiness and Complaint.

FIRST, As to their *Orders*. The *Peasant* complains aloud; the *Courtier* in Secret repines;

pines: In *Want*, what Diſtreſs? In *Affluence*, what Satiety? The G*reat* are under as much Difficulty to expend with Pleaſure, as the *Mean* to labour with Succeſs. In *Retirement*, what Oſcitancy, what Heavineſs? In the World, what Conflict, what Fatigue? The *Ignorant*, thro' ill-grounded Hope, are diſappointed; the *Knowing*, thro' Knowledge, deſpond. Ignorance occaſions Miſtake; Miſtake Diſappointment, and Diſappointment *is* Miſery: Knowledge, on the other Hand, gives true Judgment: and true Judgment of Things below, gives a Demonſtration of their Inſufficiency to our Peace. *Good Fortune* makes the Will undiſciplined and diſſolute, the Imagination vain, the Paſſions ſtrong, and the Underſtanding weak: A miſerable State! *Affliction* is the beſt School of Wiſdom; no Volumes are an Equivalent for the Neceſſity of Reflection *that* lays us under; but then it muſt be confeſſed we pay dear for its Inſtruction: And ſince the End of Wiſdom is to lead us to Pleaſure, what ſignifies that Wiſdom which is accompanied with Pain?

THE *Marriage State* only *may* be the moſt happy, but *is* the moſt dangerous; as fruitful of Calamities, as it is of Relations; whoſe Capacity of being our greateſt Pleaſures, is likewiſe their Capacity of being our greateſt Pains. And if we conſult Experience more than Reaſon in this Point, we have Grounds to fear the worſt. Nor is Reaſon entirely on
the

the other Side; for if there are more Vices, than Virtues, more unfortunate than fortunate Accidents in Life, the Ballance, in this State, will probably turn against us: The *Good* in it we look on as our Due, and therefore receive it coldly, and without a proper Emotion of Heart; the *Bad* is unexpected, and therefore keen the Resentment of it: The Shaft is sharp; the Surprize dips it in Poison, and doubles our Anguish. But Parties look on all that the other can do for them as an absolute *Debt*: This Notion leaves Both a much less Power to *oblige*, than to *disgust*; and consequently makes Disquiets almost unavoidable.

THE *State of Celebacy*, unless it can work out an *artificial* Happiness for the Absence of Evils, which requires a peculiar Strength of Mind, is a desert, melancholy, and disconsolate State: At the Maturity of Life, tender Affections awake in the Heart, which demand their proper Objects, and pine for the want of them. In this State of Celebacy, they must either be extinguished, or continued without Gratification: The *first* is a great Violence to Nature; the *second*, her lasting Pain; and a Pain of that Kind, which furnished the *Platonists* with their principal Idea of Hell. Our Paternal *Affections* must be drawn off, like a Mother's *Milk*, or they will corrupt, and turn to Disease.

HUSBAND, and *Father*, are the Titles of Honour which *Nature* dispenses, and endows

dows them with greater Pleasure, than any Titles which *Fortune* can confer. They that resist the Impulses of Nature, are resisted by Her, in their *new* Schemes of Enjoyment; and Nature is a powerful Adversary. He that has Children *multiplies* himself, and gives Happiness many Channels by which to flow in upon him: Letting the Heart stream out in Tenderness on its proper Objects, as it is the greatest Duty, so it is the greatest Blessing of Life: To have no one, to whom we heartily wish well, and for whom we are warmly concerned, is a deplorable State. It may be said, that *Wisdom* will provide us with such Objects, in every Condition: It may; but it would cost us less Pains, if we suffered *Nature* to ease her of that Trouble.

PERSONS of *Birth*, *Riches*, *Power*, and *Talents*, those shining, and envied Characters, have all their *peculiar* Evils, the Growth of their respective States.

FIRST, Persons of *Birth*: These have their Eye on their Ancestors; and would have their *Glory* subsist on the *Merit* of the Dead. This the World will not agree to, but thinks That an *Argument* for Attainments of their own, which the Great by Birth look on as their *Exemption* from the Labour of them: Thus are they pain'd, where they expect *Homage*, to find *Reproach*. They contemn those of mean Extraction; and by that Contempt, as it were, *exact* their Hate; and generally *have*
what

what they exact, with the bad Consequences of it. Ardently they desire Honours, because it is natural to Men to desire an *Accumulation* of that *Good*, of which already they enjoy a Share: Hence a Disappointment in *This* Pursuit, is more stinging to them, than others. Who is *truly* more noble for his high Birth? He that despises it: He that despises it as a *Possession*, but values it as an *Incitement* to Virtue. Their *Appellations* are their *Instructors*; they are stiled *Noble*, on a Presumption that they retain the *Virtue*; their Blood is stiled *Generous*, on a Presumption that they retain the *high Nature*, of their Ancestors. Their *Riches* are not sufficient.

SECONDLY, Men of *Riches:* These Men, which is natural, are so high in their Opinion of what they largely possess, that they think to have *Riches*, is to have *every Thing*; that, they think them the *Price* for, and *Title* to All the World can give, or Man enjoy. Hence high *Expectations*, and high *Resentments*, and every Evil is aggrandized by These. Every wrong Accident is a *Calamity*, and not only a Calamity, but an *Injury* too; for have not *They* a Title to better Things? Others, when they are sick, are *sorry*; but these are *angry* also, and look on a *Gout*, or a *Fever*, as an Object of *Resentment*; which is still the stranger, because, for the most Part, they *invite* them to their Habitations.

THIRDLY,

THIRDLY, Men of *Power:* They that have it in their Power to make the Fortune, and Reputation of others, *may* have, and often have as many Enemies, as those whose Fortune, and Reputation they do *not* make. For Men are so fond of themselves, as to think that All others *can* do, they *should do* for them. This is unjust, but this is true. And hence it is, that all the *Uneasy,* instead of venting their Passion by striking the Air, as it is natural for the Peevish in their Gusts of Rage to do, vent it often on Men in Power, by shooting their Arrows at them, *even bitter Words;* Because Men are apt to think they contract an Importance, from the Importance of those they injure. Whereas 'tis rare that Men in Power give just Offence to such as these: If they injure, they stoop not to these; they level at the Great, for that gives their *Dignity* the highest Satisfaction. The *Great* often *justly are,* the *Mean* often, *unjustly will be,* their Enemies. Where then are their Friends? They must be few; and those few are more likely to be secret Enemies to Them, than to any others with whom they pass for Friends. Because, First, Men of Power create the greatest *Envy,* which is our *strongest Passion:* Secondly, their Ruin would afford the largest Plunder, and our own Emolument is our *chiefest Aim.*

FOURTHLY, Men of *Talents:* If they do not exert them, it will cost them much
Pains

Pains, and they may probably fail of Succefs, through *Malice* of *Accident*, or *Indifcretion* of *Choice*. Or if they fucceed in their *Labour*, their Labour may not fucceed in its Reputation; or if it does, it is only fetting themfelves a *hard Task* for the future; for it is *double* Shame to fall beneath themfelves. *Fame* is generally Thefe mens Aim; and to fail of our Aim, be it never fo idle, is Infelicity. An Author at his Lamp tells himfelf in Triumph, now the Toil is almoft over, the Purchafe at hand, he's within a Month of Immortality. But on *Publication* he finds the Payment deferred; deferr'd to the Day of his Death; too late a Payment of *That* which he cannot transfer to his Heir. There is no ftronger Infatuation than this Defire of chimerical Immortality. It is very ftrange; but the Secret of it is this: God implanted in the Soul a violent Defire of *Approbation*, in order to ftimulate Men into an Attainment of his own Approbation, which is the moft valuable; as he implanted in the Soul ftrong *Hope*, and *Fear*, and *Love*, that he himfelf might be the Object of them, as my Text directs: But as thefe *Affections* when they ftop fhort on *Temporals*, become *Pains*; fo this violent Defire of *Approbation*, when it ftops fhort at Men, becomes, tho' moft admirably wife in God's Defign, that ridiculous, and feemingly unaccountable Folly of which I fpeak: And the wifeft of Men, not attending to this, have fometimes ftarted in Surprize and Shame, on difcovering that fome of their noblest Designs had their Rise, and Termination in that most despicable Point, the *Opinion of Men*. Thus you see that the Thirst of *Approbation*, when misapply'd becomes a *Folly*, and incurs *Shame*, which it would *most* avoid. And this is the State of the greatest Gifts that Omnipotence can bestow, when turned on improper Ends. *This*, therefore, which might seem *digressive*, is not so; it tends to demonstrate the Miseries of this Life, since hence it appears, that we have Reason to stand in Dread of the very *Excellencies* of our Nature, as well as the *Imperfections* of it.

SECONDLY, Consider the different *Ages*: *Young* Men desire *passionately*, and therefore are *afflictively* disappointed. They desire chiefly Gratifications of *Sense*, and therefore soon impair their Appetites for them, and anticipate old Age by Infirmities.

THEY are extreamly *mutable* in their Inclinations, and therefore as some Things by *Nature cannot*, others, through their own *Temper, shall not* please them long.

THEY are *fastidious* in their Pleasures, as thinking the most delicate and exalted, the Prerogative of their Time of Life: Thus they *reject* many, and *impair* the rest.

THEY are *prone to Anger*, because unsubdued by *Fortune*, and unapprized by *Wisdom* of what they ought to expect: Hence are they

they difpleafed with others without Caufe, and then with themfelves, for being fo; for generally their *Senfe* of being in the Wrong is as quick, as their Propenfity to it, is ftrong.

THEY have not a fufficient Regard for Things of *Utility*, (becaufe they never wanted,) and find the bad Effects of it; what Pride can better tafte, pleafes Them more: Hence they are very *tender of their Honour*, before they have gained any; and *thus* are they pain'd, not only about Things that *are*, but Things alfo, that *are not*.

THEY are *credulous*, becaufe unexperienced; deceived, becaufe credulous; and outrageous, becaufe deceived: And hence, from *too fond an Opinion*, they are apt to conceive *too inveterate a Diflike* for Mankind; as fruitful a Source of Evil, as their *firft* Miftake.

THE young Man's Field of *Reflection* is fmall, for little is paft; his Field of *Hope* large, for much is to come; which falling in with Vivacity of Spirits, and Vanity of Heart, he indulges it to the Exclufion of neceffary Fear, which is the Shield of Life; and hence is he perpetually wounded in his *Peace, Fortune, Reputation*, or *Health*, or All.

HE delights in *Extreams*, whereas *Virtue* is in the *Mean*, and Happinefs dwells with her. He is a Squanderer of *Wealth*, as well as of Health, Peace, and Reputation; and by the

D 2   Guilt

Guilt of Youth, lays up *Poverty* for Age; of which I am now to speak.

AGE is infested with *Suspicion, Excess of Caution, Disaffection, Pusilanimity, Illiberality, Querulousness, Immodesty, Garrulity, Want of Compassion, solid Hatred, Moroseness, inordinate Self-Love, extream Covetousness,* and *Distempers.*

AN *old Man* is *suspicious*, because incredulous; and incredulous, because experienced. For the *Knowledge*, and *Distrust* of Mankind are inseparable. Now he that lives in perpetual *Suspicion*, lives the Life of a Centinel, of a Centinel never relieved; whose Business it is to *look out* for, and *expect* an Enemy, which is an Evil not very far short of *perishing by him*.

ALLIED to Suspicion is *Excess of Caution:* Wisdom, Coldness of Temperature, and sometimes Ill-nature, are mixed in this. I shall chuse one Instance that includes them all: In Points of Speculation he rarely affirms, or denies any Thing positively, though *he* is best able to do it: He *knows* nothing, but is of *such an Opinion* on most Occasions; by which, one Thing he means, is, to call younger Men Fools, (who delight in a more sanguine Stile) and thus, artfully, to gratify his Disaffection to them.

HE is all *Disaffection:* I speak in general. He loves no body, because formerly, very probably,

probably, his good Inclinations have been abused; besides, the Affections as naturally contract in the Evening of Life, as Flowers at the Departure of the Sun. Now he that loves none, enjoys none; nor is lov'd, or enjoyed by any.

HE is *Pusilanimous*, from Decay of Spirits, and the Blows of Fortune. Now Pusilanimity is the Want of *Hope*, and Hope is the *Cordial* of Life.

HE is *Querulous*, which is the Voice of Pusilanimity; and an infallible Source of *Contempt*.

HE is *Illiberal*, as knowing how hard it is to *gain*, and how easy to *lose*; as likewise, from a growing Passion for the Security of *To-morrow*; whereas *To-Day* is the Mistress of Youth. Now Illiberality is the Source of *Hatred*, as *Generosity* is of Love.

HE is *Immodest*, I mean hardened to the Eye, and unaffected with the Opinion of others, because he disesteems them; and disesteems them, because he knows them; and Praise, and Dispraise we disesteem, when we disesteem Those from whom they come. Now this Immodesty is a Source both of *Hatred*, and *Contempt*. Besides, *Virtue* is always enfeebled by a Neglect of Praise, which is a Food of it.

HE

HE is *Talkative*, becaufe his largeſt Scene lies *backward* ; and his Talk on the *paſt*, is always a Cenſure on the *preſent :* Now he that cenſures, is *diſpleaſed.* Befides, *this* Talkativeneſs is difguſting on two Accounts: Firſt, as he is generally his own Theme; Secondly, as it runs counter to the Fire, and Activity of younger Men, to whom he ſpeaks.

HIS *Compaſſion* is *ſlight*, from his Familiarity with Misfortunes; and his *Hatred* is *ſolid*, more apt to vent it ſelf in *Deeds* than *Words*, from the Maturity of his Wiſdom, which loves Things *effectual*, and to the Purpoſe. His *former* Qualities put him in a State of War with Mankind: *This*, in a State of War that gives no Quarter.

HE is *Moroſe*, and an *inordinate Lover of himſelf.* The *Firſt*, becauſe he envies Pleaſures which he can't partake. There is no ſuch Thing, at leaſt, in our Climate, as a gay old Man; A *Fly in Winter* is for Nations nearer the Sun. He is the *Second*, becauſe Men riſe in Fondneſs for Things, in Proportion to their Hazard of loſing them; and his Life is on the Departure. Hence abſurdly his *Paſſion* for it increaſes, as its *Value* fails. Now from all that has been ſaid,

HIS *extream Covetouſneſs* is accounted for. Money has *two* excellent Qualities for him: *Firſt*, it will do that for him, which no one will, willingly, do: It will keep him Company,

pany, as it always does; it will flatter him; it will go on his Errands; it will procure him Smiles, and Bows, and all the *Outside* of Affection, and Respect. *Secondly*, as it is a Thing *inanimate*, it can give no Offence. But not to aggravate this Matter, (which it little needs!) granting, that as *Youth* is the Reign of vehement Desire, and vehement Desire, is a Disease, a Fever, a Pain; so *Age*, indeed, brings on a Serenity; *Experience* makes us able Pilots in the Waves of Fortune, and *Vigour impair'd* no longer scorches us with the Violence of Desire; Granting, that the Mind gains that Strength which the Body loses, and intellectual Pleasures are then in their full Force; yet so, it must be confess'd, are

DISTEMPERS too; and what Comfort is there in an *Hospital*, or a *Storm?* In *Youth* what Disappointments of our own making? In *Age* what Disappointments from the Nature of Things? It is long before we arrive at a right Conduct, and by that at a true Relish, and good Husbandry of Life; and when we are arrived at it, as much as *Wisdom* gives, *Time* withdraws, Objects begin to flatten, and Appetites to fail. Human Life has then its Morning and Evening; but *the Evening and Morning are one Day;* a Day of Sorrows! different indeed in Sort, but in Essence the same. And *this* is the Reason why Men always unhappy, are always expecting Happiness. For had we no Change of Scenes

Scenes to experience one after another, we should sooner be convinced of the Vanity of our Expectations: Whereas we, now, are amused with Hope, which, for Pleasure, gives us Change of Pain; we are *wretched*, and *deceived*, which increases our Wretchedness; for every Sorrow receives a new Sting, from our Expectation of the contrary.

THIRDLY, Consider our *Aims:* If we let loose our Wishes at Things above our Desert, how rarely we succeed? Or if we succeed, how are we pain'd with the Fears of exposing our Insufficiency? How shall we make good the Promise our *Fortune* has made to the World? We must live in perpetual Constraint; be for ever sweating under a Mask of Form and Artifice, which, in spite of all our Care, the Wise will see through; and, at their Mercy we lie, for the precarious Character we preserve. And how ridiculous a Sight it is, to see a Man embarrass'd by good Fortune, and struggling with his own Success? To take up more Money than our *Estate* can answer, in Time, is certain *Ruin:* To take up more Reputation than our *Merit* can answer, in Time, is as certain *Shame*.

IF our *Fortune*, on the other hand, falls below our *Desert*, how careless are we of exerting those Capacities we are really Masters of, and of levying that Advantage, and Reputation which is due to them? Our Preferment is our Punishment; and the Consciousness

ness of our Worth is at once our *Pride*, and our *Affliction*; How unpromising a Scene is *that* for Happiness, where our Merit increases the Number of our Pains?

IF our Aims are *proportion'd* to our *Desert*, we may indeed succeed; but our Success will soon grow insipid, nay, painful, when we see (as soon we shall!) our Inferiors in Merit get the Start of us in Place, and Fortune; when we find our *Wisdom*, and *Modesty* less advantageous, than the *Rashness*, and *Confidence* of other Men.

IF we stand *Alone*, and Independent, it is a proud, but a solitary, and uncomfortable Dominion; unrefresh'd with Hope, which is the Life of Life itself. If we have our Attachments, and lean against our Superiors, it is often a shining Servitude, a promising Anxiety, that excites indeed our Spirits, but torments them too, during the *Suspence*; and as often deceives, as satisfies, in the *End*. Which has most Happiness? a servile Hope, or a hopeless Independency? He that has Many *Hopes*, has many Possibilities of *Disappointment*; He that has few, has few Occasions of *Joy*.

IF we converse with our *Inferiors*, or *Equals* only, we sacrifice the Advancement of our Fortune, to present Ease and Complacency; If with our *Superiors*, we in some Measure sacrifice our Ease, and Complacency, to our Fortune; our Caution must be always awake,

awake, our Abilities always on the Stretch; and Conversation, which was designed to re-*create*, must become a Discipline, and an Enterprize.

MOREOVER, it is *Expectation* from Superiors that is apt to give a painful, and unreasonable Awe of them; an Awe due rather to God, than Man. It is *That* which annoys our Breasts with pusilanimous Doubts, and Fears; *That* makes the little Heart play its servile Passions in all their Force, at a Smile, or a Frown; which He that does *not expect*, is free from himself, and in others, most justly contemns. The most despicable Weakness any one Man can be guilty of, is an undue Fear of another, which *Expectation* is apt to subject him to.

OBSCURITY has its obvious Disadvanges; and a *Great Name* is the Mark of Envy, and Reproach: Or if Reproach spare it, it must be Nurtur'd, or Lost. *Time* itself will work Decay in Glory, as in other Things; unless it be kept in Repair at the Expence of returning Pains, and a Succession of Deserts: And if preserved, it has its *moral* Evils; Fame from *Letters* makes a Man unsociable, and overbearing; Fame from political Wisdom, designing; and Fame from *Arms*, incorrect of Life. It has likewise its *natural* Evils. For since *Fame* is the general Mistress of Mankind, he that enjoys it has almost as many Rivals as Men, and often as many Foes, as Rivals.

ONE

ONE Man aims at making his Happiness by *Philosophy*, another by *Fortune*. The *First* is stemming the Stream of the World, and his own Nature, with endless Labour; the *Second* is carried away by That stream, with endless Hazard, and every Wave is Master of his Peace.

ONE follows *Fancy*, and by that Time the Thing fancied is attained, his Fancy for it is fled. Another follows *Custom*, and is fashionably pleased in Contradiction to his own Heart. Seeming to be happy, is his Happiness; now *seeming* Happiness implies the *Want* of it. A third follows *Reason*; and Reason puts us out of Humour with almost every Thing about us.

IF Men have no *Pursuits* they are a Burthen to themselves; if they have, Disappointments are a Greater. What Disappointments interrupt the most successful *Prosecutions*? And what is worse, *Possession* is the greatest Disappointment of all; it destroys the very Phantom of Happiness, our pleasing Error, our sweet Flatterer, Hope, which before we enjoyed. The Man of Success, and of the highest Advancement, first indeed laughs at others; but soon he revenges them, by laughing at *himself*. He wonders how he could be so passionately fond of what so little deserved his Fondness: He is grieved, he is surprized, he is angry, that the Absence of those Things was able to give him so much Pain, the Presence of which can afford so little Enjoyment. But he usually keeps the Secret, in poor Hopes of That enjoyment from the mistaken Envy of others, which the Things Envied cannot give him; and takes a malicious Pleasure in seeing his unwarned Followers deceived, as well as himself. There is ever a certain Languor attending the Fulness of Prosperity: When the Heart has no more to wish, it yawns over its Possession; and the Energy of the Soul goes out, like a Flame that has no more to devour; or, like a Storm, loses its Force for want of Opposition. Who is so wretched as the Man that is overwhelm'd with a Multitude of Affairs? He that is relieved from them, and has none at all. But granting Superiority of Fortune should give some Superiority of Happiness, let it be remarked, that he who increases the Endearments of Life, increases, at the same Time, the Terrors of Death. Which leads me to

THE *Fourth* Consideration, that of our *Relations* in Life: A Wife, a Child, dear to us as our own Bosoms in which they lie, what Cowards do they make us? What are their Endearments, their Softness, their Charms, but new Terrors in the Frown, and new Shafts in the Quiver of *Misfortune*, and *Death*? There is something truly Formidable in having such tender Blessings as these; and every wife, and

A true Estimate of Human Life. 29

and feeling Heart, while it is transported at the Thoughts of them, must tremble too.

BUT all Relations are not pain'd through Tenderness of Affection. While the Father is sollicitous for the Welfare of his Son, how sollicitous and impatient is the Son (very often) for the Death of that very Father? What are Alliances of Blood, but Titles for Expectation? And what are Titles for Expectation, but Exposures *to* Disappointment, and Aggravations *of* its Smart? All That seeming Family-endearment, Comfort, and Complacency, which we figure to our selves at a Distance, what is it, (too often!) but mutual Attacks on the Peace, Plots on the Riches, Hopes from the Sickness, and Joy from the Deaths of each other?

THE Servant envies his Master, and sometimes the Master his Servant, and perhaps with more Justice; but justly, neither. For if we well knew how little others enjoy, it would rescue the World from one Sin, there would be no such Thing as Envy upon Earth; Envy, which is a *double* Folly; Folly, as it is a Sin, and Folly as it is a Mistake; for it results from the Supposition of that which is not, the superior Happiness of others; which is not, I mean, in that Degree we conceive of it; and we *envy* That which we *conceive*.

FIFTHLY, As to *Constitutions*, and *Tempers:* In Health, what Temptation? In Sickness,

Sickness, what Pain? The Misery of many is wrap'd up in their very Veins, how then shall they fly from it? How many inherit, how many create, how many purchase Distempers? Earthquake, Storm, War, sweep not half so many, as Diseases which we knowingly, contract by Carelesness, and Excess. Women, as they are less subject to Pains of Mind, are more subject to Pains of the Body than Men, to ballance that Account.

HE that is infirm, dies daily, and loses all the Pleasure of *Life:* He that knows no Infirmities, observes not the Lapse of Time, grows old unawares, and is unprepar'd for *Death:* But suppose a Man has Health, and Wisdom too, how many find in their *Tempers* an Enemy to Peace?

THE *Tempers* are, as I take it, lesser *Passions,* or, various fainter *Shades,* or *Blendings* of Those strong *Colours* on the Soul of Man. The *Gloomy, Peevish, Sanguine, Phlegmatick, Good-natur'd, Impatient, Improvident, Wary, Haughty, Remitting, Courteous, Arrogant, Suspicious, Refining, Reserved, Affable, Fearless, Timid, Modest, Proud, Delicate,* and *Insensible* Temper, have all their peculiar Evils.

A *gloomy* Temper surveys every Thing in the worst Light, and can discover no Blessings.

A *peevish* Temper quarrels with the Blessings it discovers, with its Friends, itself; and
defeats

defeats the Labour of Providence for its Satiffaction.

THE *Sanguine* overshoots; the *Phlegmatick* desponds; the *Mild* tempts Insults; the *Cholerick* is its own Tormentor.

IF a Man is *Good-natur'd*, his Friends devour him; if not, his Foes.

THE *Impatient* feels as much Uneasiness from the *slow* Approach of Pleasure, as Others from the Despair of it.

TO the *Thoughtless*, and *Improvident*, the *Surprize* of every Disappointment doubles its Pain.

TO the *Wary*, and *Foreboding*, the constant Expectation of Calamity, is a Calamity itself.

IF a Man is *Haughty*, and too tender of his Honour, he gives the Power of hurting him to every Wretch that can shew Disrespect: And who cannot? If He is remiss, and negligent of Respect, Men will withhold *real Services*, because their *Ceremonial* was not sufficiently welcome; He loses the Substance, because he will *not* catch at the Shadow. But *Forms* are more than Shadows, they are the Robe, and Defence of *Realities*, which will ever run some Hazard, when we throw them off.

THE *very Courteous* lessen their Favours by giving them the Appearance of a Debt, thro'

thro' their frequent Professions of Kindness: The Favours of an *arrogant* Man are received unthankfully; because, thro' too great a Consciousness of them, he is his own Pay-Master. And yet he who does not sometimes assert his own Merit, will soon have painful Suspicions that the *Former* is in the Right.

THE *Suspicious*, in some measure, justify those Injuries, they *expect*. A Person of small Merit is anxiously *jealous* of Imputations on his Honour, because he knows his Title is *weak*; one of great Merit turbidly *resents* them, because he knows his Title is *strong*.

THE *Refining* Temper is expresly a *Maker of Evils*: Not to be obliged by Superiors, It construes an Injury; to be obliged by Inferiors, an Affront. To have its Wants relieved, It construes an Affectation of Superiority in its Benefactor; not to have them relieved, a Contempt. It can work Wonders to its own Disadvantage, and make a *Look*, or *Gesture*, it disapproves, a *serious* Misfortune.

RESERVE may procure Respect, but it gives a Disposition to Hatred; because That Respect is involuntary, and as it were, extorted; and we hate every Thing that invades the Freedom of our Choice.

AFFABILITY procures Good-will, but may give a Disposition to Contempt; because it gives us cheaply that which we desire, and the

A true Estimate of Human Life.

the Difficulty of the Attainment enhances the Value of Things.

A *Fearless* Temper impairs our Caution, and makes us careless of exerting our utmost Strength; A *Timid*, gives our *Understanding* the strongest Arguments for exerting our Strength, but at the same Time enfeebles the Heart in the Execution of what appears so reasonable.

A *Native Modesty* in Men may conciliate *Love* from the *Many*, but forbids *Esteem* from the *Wise:* Because with them no Act has Merit, but what has Choice; and these *chuse* not Modesty by their *Reason*, but *suffer* it from their *Constitutions*.

PROUD Men are apt to be injurious, because it is a *Mark* of Superiority: They strike more through Vanity, than Malice; but then, as it is a *Mark*, it is a Mutulation of Superiority too; For it throws down our Respect for them, which is a considerable Support of it.

TOO great a Sensibility creates Pain, where by Nature it is not; too *little* perceives not Blessings where they are: And there is a too great Sensibility from *Fortune*, as well as *Temper:* Rank gives some Persons such a Delicacy, that they have a Set of Inquietudes entirely their own, the Prerogative of their high Station, to which their Inferiors must not presume to pretend. If *Humour*, and *Passion*

Paſſion are indulged, how domineering are they? If denied, how rebellious? which leads me to

THE Sixth and laſt Conſideration, the *Paſſions* of Men.

AN Account of the *Paſſions* is properly a Hiſtory of the *Active* Part of the Soul, as an Account of the *Underſtanding* is of the *Contemplative*. They may be conſider'd as ſo many *Standard-Bearers*, round each of which many Miſchiefs are rang'd in array againſt us, and lay waſte the Tranquility of Human Life. They have by others been conſider'd *Phyſically*, as they conſtitute Part of our Nature; *Morally*, as they influence Virtue and Vice; and *Rhetorically*, with regard to Compoſition; But I do not know that they have been conſider'd in a Syſtem, or with any Accuracy, as the *Pains*, and *Promoters of the Pains* of Life. In this View I ſhall ſpeak of them, with as much Light, and Diſtinction, as I can. It is the Paſſions that give the *perpetual Motion* to Human Life, that roll us from Place to Place, from Object to Object, nor will the Grave it ſelf afford them Reſt.

FIRST, *Anger*. It is elegantly ſay'd, *the King's Anger is as a Roaring Lyon*. Which Deſcription of it is confin'd to Kings, only as to its Efficacy; it is as *ſtrong*, tho' not as *ſucceſsful* in other Men. By a King it is let loſe into the large Field of Power, in others

others it bites the Bars that confine it, and, in both, it lashes it self. This shows it to be a *Pain*; and it likewise proceeds from Pain; for no one is angry, but who has, or fancies he has received an Injury in himself, or *His*; for which he is, first, Grieved. So that Anger may be called the Daughter of *Sorrow*, and the Mother of *Revenge*, which often has fatal Consequences. Thus this Passion has *past*, *present*, and *future* Pains belonging to it.

ANGER is frequent; for among Enemies it is the *natural* Habit of the Mind; and where are not Enemies? Among Friends, it is *unnatural*, and therefore, when it happens, more tormenting.

AS Pride is *predominant* in Man, the principal Cause of Anger is Disrespect; the Question therefore is, if the angry Man acts not against his own supream Purpose: If Anger is *impotent*, That is a Blow directly on his *Pride*; if it succeeds by unworthy Means, That is a Blow on his general Character. Anger therefore is not only an Evil it self, proceeding *from*, and leading *to* Evil, but, often, to the very Evil it would most avoid. It falls on its own Sword.

TWO Sorts of Men are most subject to this Passion; Men of *Felicity*, and Men of *Affliction*. One because their *Expectations* are high, the other because their *Uneasinesses* are many. The *First* make their Superiority their Anxiety, counterballancing by their own Resentment, the *Favours* of Nature, and Fortune; the *Second* inflame the *Severities* of them both.

ALLY'D to Anger is *Hatred*, which is a lasting Anger; now Hatred is always accompany'd with Disgust, and Disgust is Pain.

ALLY'D to Hatred are *Contempt*, and *Abhorrence*; Contempt is Hatred without Fear, but it is *Hatred*, and therefore Pain. *Abhorrence* is Hatred with Fear, and therefore its Pain is double.

INVECTIVE indeed eases the Heart, as a Discharge the Stomach, but It also proves it very sick before.

I DO not deny that there is such a Thing as a malicious *Pleasure*; but I affirm it is a Pleasure like that of violent scratching, or striking our selves in some Dispositions; It supposes a Distemper, and leaves a Wound, both in our Reputation, and our Peace.

ANGER has under its Banner, *Invective*, *Assault*, *Ruin*, and *Death*.

SECONDLY, *Love*. By Love I mean not the Desire of what is *Useful*, or *Honest*, but more particularly of what is *Pleasant*. With *Philosophers* it includes the *two Former*, with the *World* it is often limited to the *Last*. It implies Discontent, that is *Pain*; for he that desires, is dissatisfy'd with his present Condition,

A true Estimate of Human Life. 37

Condition, be it what it will. And the Pain is in Proportion to the Desire.

TO say the least to the Disadvantage of this Passion. It is putting your Peace in the Power of *another*, which is rarely safe even in your *own*.

THERE are *Two* Things, I think, *peculiar* to this Passion, and what makes them more remarkable, is, they seem somewhat inconsistent. *One* is our *Desire* of it; the *Other* is a Condition That makes it very *Undesirable*. As to the First, we don't seek, nay, we avoid Occasions of *Anger*, *Hatred*, *Fear*, *Shame*, or *Envy*, but we seek Occasions of *Love*. As to the Second, Love is *all* the Passions in *one:* It is *Anger* that it *cannot*, *Shame* that it *does not*, *Fear* that it *shall not* enjoy its Object; It is *Envy* of, and *Hatred* to, those that possibly may. For *Envy*, *Hatred*, and *Suspicion* form Loves constant Companion, *Jealousie*; which therefore stings deeper than *either* of them, because it is *all*. Now as many Passions as Love has, so many Pains. Be it therefore a Maxim, He that was never *Pain'd*, never *Lov'd*.

BUT tho' this Passion has Pains, leads it not to *Pleasures?* It *may* fail of them, and then it is *Despair*, which is most terrible; If it attains them, they may not be lasting; For most Pleasures, like Flowers, when gather'd, die.

LOVE

LOVE has under its Banner, *Watching, Sickness, Abasement, Adulation, Perjury, Jealousie*; and sometimes It lifts *Anger's* most dreadful Followers; the only difference is, *there*, they are standing Troops, *here*, casual Recruits; there, they are *Voluntiers*, here, they are *Pressed* occasionally into the Service, for they do not *naturally* belong to Love.

THIRDLY, *Fear*. This is a most dismal Passion; a Mind haunted with Fear is a hideous Night-Piece of Storm, Precipice, Ruins, Tombs, and Apparitions; It is not content with the Compass of Nature, as if too scanty for Evil, but creates new Worlds for Calamity; Things that are *not*. But *very timorous* Natures only suffer to this Degree; and it is well they do not; For *such a Fear* alone is capable of taking in an ample Vengeance of an Incens'd God. Insomuch that some have thought that Hell consisted in the severe Extremity of this Passion only.

ALL, that *Fear*, have proportionable *Pain*. It is an Anticipation of Evil; and has under its Banner, *Confusion, Supplication, Servility, Amazement*, and *Self-Desertion* particularly.

FOR I think it a *Peculiarity* of *Fear* that it defeats its own Purpose more than any of the Passions. *Anger* strikes, and if unsuccessfully, it only loses a Blow; *Love* pursues,

purſues, and if unſuccefsfully, it only loſes a Purſuit; *Fear* makes us fly, but makes us ſtumble too, and the more precipitate our Flight, the farther are we from an Eſcape. Hence ſays the Holy Scripture, *It betrays the Succours of Reaſon*, meaning, that it betrays it more than any other Paſſion, for all betray it in ſome Degree.

FEARS are the *Shields* of Life; but if they are too many, they are an Oppreſſion, and like the Maid at the *Capitol*, we periſh under them.

FEARS we have many, but there is *but one that came from Heaven*, (as the *Romans* fabled of their *Ancile*,) which is the Fear of God; *All the reſt are falſe*; and This ſevenfold Shield will ſave us from them: A Falling World can not affright Him, whom That ſhield has under its Protection.

FOURTHLY, There is alſo *Falſe Shame*; When, thro' an Affectation of the Eſteem of bad Men, we are aſham'd of what God approves; or if aſham'd of what is truly ſhameful, when, we are aſham'd with regard to Men, not God. The *Firſt* is Blaſphemy in thought; or ſuch a Thought, as if expreſs'd in Words, would be Blaſphemous. The *Second* is Sacriledge, giving God's Due to Man. This is a Shame to be aſham'd of; and *contrary* to the Apoſtle's
Repentance

Repentance not to be repented of, for Shame is a Repentance, or something very like it.

SHAME is a Sense of Estimation impair'd, and of our sinking in the Opinion of *Men*; I wish I could add of *God* too; for Men are not asham'd of *Injustice*, or *Prophaneness*, at the same Time that they blush for an Omission in *Fashion*, or *Complaisance:* Nay I wish they are not often *Proud* of the *Former*; now Pride is *Shame*'s Reverse. As shining in the Opinion of others is the supream Aim of almost all Men, *Shame* must be exceeding *Painful*, as it implies the Loss, or Diminution of their greatest *fancy'd* Good. Besides, every Man, while he is *asham'd* wishes his Condition *alter'd*, which no Man does that is *happy* under it.

SHAME has under its Banner, *Self-Condemnation*, *Pusilanimity*, *Regret*, *Lying*, *Confusion of Face*.

WHICH Last puts me in Mind of what I take to be *Peculiarities* of this Passion. Which are Three. First, Other Passions fly *to* Men for Redress of their Grievances, This flies *from* them: *Anger* flies to strike, *Love* to embrace, *Fear* for Shelter; But Shame flies from all Men, and makes an Eye as sharp as a Sword. Shame's bad Estate is seen in this, that its Hope, and Felicity runs so low, as to make *Night*, and *Oblivion*,

Oblivion, which are the Terror of others, a Wish, a Joy; *Fallere & Effugere est Triumphus.* So that it robs Man of one of his most Essential good Qualities, that of his being a *sociable* Creature.

SECONDLY, *Shame* has a more Infallible *Mark* fix'd on it by Nature, than any of the rest, I mean Blushes. Of which I take the Reason to be, that this Passion *necessarily* supposes *Guilt*. Which is not the Case of any of the Passions beside, except Envy, which is generally mark'd with *Paleness*, as Shame with the Contrary. Shame, I say, necessarily supposes Guilt. For none are asham'd but on one of these Three Accounts. First Because, they are *directly* Guilty. Secondly, Because they want some Merit they ought to have. Thirdly, Because they suffer some Indignity. Now the Want of proper Merit proceeds generally from *Omissions*; suffering Indignities, from *Sloth*, or *Cowardice*; And all these are *Vicious*. But Men are sometimes asham'd of *Virtue*. True; but then they consider That Virtue as a Fault, in the Eyes of Those before whom they are asham'd of it: Besides, then, it does not only *suppose*, but *is* Guilt.

THIRDLY, *Lying*. This is the False Cover of *False* Shame; for true or proper Shame has Regard to God, and who *dares*, who *can* lye to Him? For we cannot lye to any Purpose, but to Fallible Beings. Now as *false* Shame is lying eternally, tho' the Person subject to it is asham'd without Reason *at first*, He is sure to have ample Reason for Shame *in the End*; and consequently He will be *Pain'd* without just Cause, and with it, too.

FIFTHLY, *Envy*. This is the most *Deformed*, and most *Detestable* of all the Passions. A good Man may be *Angry*, or *Asham'd*, may *Love*, or *Fear*; but a good Man can not *Envy*. For all other Passions seek Good, but *Envy Evil*. All other Passions propose *Advantages* to themselves; Envy seeks the *Detriment* of Others. *They* therefore are *Human*. *This* is *Diabolical*. *Anger* seeks Vengeance for an Injury; an Injury in Fortune, or Person, or Honour; But Envy pretends no Injuries, and yet has an Appetite for Vengeance: *Love* seeks the Possession of *Good*, *Fear* the flight of *Evil*, but Envy neither; All her Good is the Disadvantage of Another. Hence it is most Detestable; and because most Detestable, therefore, Secondly,

MOST *Deformed*. For it is the most *Detestable*, because the least *Natural*; or what is least Natural works in us the most disadvantageous, and deforming Effects. We must be sometimes *Angry*, we must *Love*, and *Fear*, and be *Ashamed* by the Necessity of our Nature, and there are just Occasions for them all. But no Necessity of of our Nature, obliges us to *Envy*, nor is there any juſt Occaſion for it. For all Men are unhappy, only we know not where their Uneaſineſs lies; therefore there is no *Natural* Occaſion for Envy; and that there ſhould be a *Moral* one is a Contradiction; for the Happier Others are, the more we ſhould *rejoice*. As therefore neither our *Nature*, nor *Reaſon* requires Envy, it is properly *Unnatural*, and becauſe Unnatural, it works ſuch terrible Effects in us. How Pale, Keen, Inhuman, and Emaciated is it's Look, if the undeſerved Indulgence of Conſtitution gets not the better of thoſe Effects? Now all theſe are Demonſtrations of its extream *Pain*.

MEN of Imagination therefore have been fond of this Subject, as Painters, Poets, Hiſtorians, for the Imagination delights in *Extreams*; and nothing is more terrible than their Deſcriptions of it, but the Thing it ſelf. *A chearful Heart does good like a Medicine*, but Envy corrodes like a Poiſon; It is ſo ſharp, that it cuts the Body which ſheaths it. Nay it is thought by ſome, actually to ſend forth its Virulence; to ſit Viſible in the Eyes, and wound its Object. Of this Opinion ſeems our greateſt *Engliſh* Philoſopher, who aſſigns Phyſical Reaſons why Perſons in *Joy*, and *Triumph*, are more liable to receive this Venom than Others. What a Wretch muſt the Quiver of such Arrows be? Such is the *Pain* of Envy, that it made the two Greatest, and Bravest Men that ever liv'd, Weep; It made them shed Tears, but not of Compassion, though over the Monuments of the Dead.

COMPASSION is griev'd at Others Evil, *Envy* at Others Good. *Indignation* is griev'd that the Unworthy prosper, *Envy* that the Meritorious prosper, also. *Emulation* is griev'd at its own *Wants*, *Envy* at the Enjoyments of Others. Nay it principally maligns Those who deserve the greatest Praise, (*viz.*) *New Men*, the Makers of their own Fame, and Fortune. For Rising Glory occasions the greatest Envy, as Kindling Fires, the greatest Smoak. In a Word, It is the Reverse of *Charity*; and as That is the supream Source of *Pleasure*, so This of *Pain*. This gathers Pain, as That gathers Pleasures from all the Felicities that happen to Mankind. Nor is It only *Painful*, but *Ignominious*. The most Imperfect, and Pusilanimous are most subject to it; The *First*, because their Field for Envy is largest; The *Second*, because, through Mistake, what is Little *appears* Great to *them*; and, therefore, as the proper Object of Envy.

ITS *Peculiarities* I take to be, First, That it seeks not, (as the other Passions,) Good, but Evil. Secondly, That This is

Lasting, the Others *Short*. We are Angry, or Ashamed, we Love, or Fear, for a Day, or Year; but we Envy for *Life*; and I look on it to be the most Universal Source of Unhappiness on Earth.

IT has under its Banner, *Hatred, Calumny, Treachery, Cabal,* with the *Meagerness of Famine, Venom of Pestilence,* and *Rage of War.*

NOR are the *Good,* and *Pleasurable* Passions without their Inconveniences, and Inquietudes, which is a Subject *hitherto,* I believe, unhandled. *Compassion, Indignation, Emulation, Hope,* nay and *Joy* itself, if fairly examined, will prove This true, without any Refinement, or Affectation of *novelty* in the Attempt.

FIRST, *Compassion,* while it has others Misery in its *Eye,* It has its own in its *Apprehension*; and is struck with a quick Sense of the *Obnoxious* Condition of Human Nature. Hence is it evident, that *Fear,* and *Sorrow,* are included in it; and can there be *Fear,* and *Sorrow* without Pain?

THOUGH I know it is Disputed; I venture to affirm, That our *Compassion* for Others, is accompanied with a Concern for our Selves. And I am persuaded of This, from considering the Persons who are *most,* and who are *least* inclined to *Compassion.*

THE

THE *least Inclined*, are the *most Confirmed in*, or the *most Lost to* Happiness. The *First* are not Compassionate, because most *secure*; the *Second*, because they have *felt the worst*. Little *self-concern* being mov'd by the miserable Object in These Men, Little *Compassion* is mov'd by it, too.

THE *most Inclined* to it, are the *Timid*, and *Those who have Wives, Children, and Relations*. The *First*, because They are most liable to fear for themselves; the *Second*, because they afford Misfortune the largest Mark.

AND all are more compassionate toward their Equals in Age, Fortune, Birth, Qualifications, or Manners, than others; because the Misfortunes of *such* are a more direct Alarm of Fear for *themselves*.

SECONDLY, *Indignation*. This is a Just, and Noble Passion, and none but the Noble-Minded feel it. It is a generous Zeal for Right, an Heroick, and laudable Anger at the Prosperity of Undeservers. An Anger therefore Foreign to the Unworthy, Base, and Profligate, who can conceive no Resentment that Men, like themselves, prosper. This elevated Passion has sometimes a severer Pang than is consistent with Life. *Cato* died of it. He thought no Man worthy to triumph over Liberty, and *Rome*. And That violent Deportment shown at his *Death*, which has, *hitherto*, been wrongfully imputed to a Ferocity

city of *Temper*, was, I think, owing to This accidental *Paſſion*, which was the *Cauſe of his* Death; This Fever, This noble Inflammation of Mind, This Indignation for *Cæſar's unjuſt* Succeſs. My Conjecture clears his Character in *that Reſpect*, and makes it more conſiſtent with that Humanity which he, in a peculiar Manner, manifeſted on many Occaſions in his laudable Life, which was worthy our Emulation, though his Death was Deteſtable at the beſt.

THIRDLY, *Emulation* is an Exalted, and Glorious Paſſion, Parent of moſt Excellencies in Human Life. It is Enamour'd of all Virtue, and Accompliſhment; its generous *Food* is Praiſe; its ſublime *Profeſſion*, Tranſcendency; and the *Life* it pants after, Immortality. It kindles at all that is Illuſtrious; and as it were, lights its Torch at the Sun. *Envy* ſeeks Others Evil, *Emulation* its own Good; *Envy* repines at Excellence *without* Imitation; *Emulation* Imitates, and rejoices in it. We *Envy* often what we *cannot* arrive at, we *Emulate*, nothing but what we *can*, or think at leaſt *we can* attain. Hence the *Young*, and *Magnanimous* are moſt inflam'd with Emulation, and Emulation rather of Glory, and Virtue, than of the Goods of the *Body*, or *Fortune*, till the World effaces Nature's firſt good Impreſſions. " *Hæc imitamini*,
" ſays Tully, *per Deos immortales, hæc*
" *Ampla ſunt, hæc Divina, hæc Immortalia,*
" *hæc*

"*hæc Fama celebrantur, monumentis Anna-*
"*lium mandantur, Posteritati propagantur.*

BUT tho' Emulation is the Pursuit of the most Amiable Things, and that by Persons most amiable too, it cannot Escape; It cannot escape in a bad World, where Men judge of others by themselves, being mistaken for *Envy*, and being Treated accordingly. For it has, sometimes, such a Degree of Resemblance, as to give the *Weak* Occasion of Error, and the *Malicious* of Excuse. Thus it falls *Alieno Vulnere*; not to mention its own natural *Pain*, which is at least as uneasy to the Soul, as extream Thirst is to the Body. *Hope* and *Fear* play the Heart of *Emulation* with Violence; It has its Throbs, its Paleness, and Tremblings, when carry'd to an Height.

———— *Exultantiaque haurit
Corda Pavor pulsans, Laudumque arrecta
Cupido.*

FOURTHLY, *Hope*, and *Joy*. Hope feels the Stings of Impatience, which is often so vehemently Eager, that falling from it into the *Despair* of its Object, is sometimes a sensible Ease to the Mind. *Joy* if moderate, scarce breaks thro' the General Disquiet of Life; If Immoderate, it is a Fever, a Tumult, a Gay Delirium, a *Transport*; which signifies a Man's being beside, or beyond himself; and he that is not in Possession of himself, can but ill be said to be in Possession of any thing else:

Joy

Joy in this Case, goes beyond its Bounds, into an Enemy's Country, and becomes a *Pain*; as its Tears abundantly testify. Nor has its Tears only, but it is sometimes *Mortal*.

HENCE some, nay most Philosophers, have plac'd our *Chief Good* in Serenity, or Indolence, but this is a Mistake. Indolence, or Rest is inconsistent with our Nature, and not to be found in Heaven it self, but in a *Comparative* Sense. On the Contrary, our Heaven will consist in a Pleasing Motion, a Delightful Exertion, a Transporting Progress to all Eternity. *Annihilation* is the only *Rest* for Man. What therefore we are to aim at, I shall shew in my *Second* Discourse.

TO conclude on the *Passions*. We consist of Soul, and Body; the Passions are the Wants of the Soul, as the Appetites may be call'd the Passions of the Body. So that we are made up of *Wants*, that is of *Pains*. Who is almost ever free from one Passion, or another? And as Passions are the Pains (from which they take their very Name) so are they the Destroyers too, of our Nature. They *pain* the whole Soul, they *confound* the Memory, *make wild* the Imagination, and *hurt* the Understanding, like Ebriety, which they resemble in their Natural, and Moral ill Consequences. And because they injure the Body also, therefore has the *Physician*, as well as *Moralist*, to do with them; and interdicts them to all those who desire Length of Days. Nay, they are more Terrible than that Death which they haften; for many have fled to *That* from the Torment of them. It feems *ſtrangeſt*, at firſt Sight, that *Fear*, of all the Paſſions, ſhould put on this Appearance of Courage; but it is ſo far from it, in reality, that no *Other Paſſion* ever arriv'd at Suicide, but thro' the Suggeſtion of This Trembler, *Fear*. Men die becauſe they *Fear* Life under its preſent Ills; Whereas *True Valour* meets thoſe Ills, whatever they are, with the ſame Reſolution, with which *They* meet Death. Their Cowardice ſhews a *pale*, feeble Valour, as Darkneſs ſhews the *Moon*; but *That* Valour is nothing compar'd to the *True*, as the *moon* is nothing by *day*.

IF this Account of the Paſſions be juſt, let us turn them againſt themſelves; Let us be Angry with *Anger*, aſhamed of *Shame*, afraid of *Fear*, pity *Envy*, and moderate our Fondneſs for *Love*. For ſome are ſo Idle, Ridiculous, Shameleſs, as to court the Paſſion itſelf; and at a Time too, when They have the leaſt Probability of Succeſs. *Love*, according to the different Objects it Embraces, like a *Woman Eſpouſed*, changes its Name, and becomes *Voluptuouſneſs*, *Ambition*, *Avarice*, or *Vanity*. Thoſe Four predominant Impulſes that divide Mankind between them; That beat on us, like the Four Winds of Heaven, and keep the reſtleſs World in a perpetual Storm.

ON

ON this common Subject I shall endeavour to throw some new Light, by shewing that they all act directly counter to their own Purposes, and are the *Reverse* of That which they pretend to.

FIRST, The *Voluptuous:* Can this Man be *unhappy*, whose sole Aim is *Pleasure?* whose *Study* is the *Art*, whose *Life* is the Chase, of Delight? He may, he is, nay, he *must* be so; because his *Imagination* promises much more than *Sense* is able to pay. Hence, he is always *disappointed*; but, through Ignorance or Negligence of the Cause of it, though always *disappointed*, he is always *expecting*; and repeated Experience serves only to *upbraid*, not *correct* his Conduct. And it *must* be so; for as every new Scene of Voluptuousness is a new *Light* to his Understanding, to shew the Insufficiency of *those Scenes* to his Happiness; so is it, also, a new *Blow* to his Understanding, and the Rectitude of his Will, and weakens his Power of resisting *Them*. Hence is he reduced to the wretched State of eternally *pursuing*, and eternally *condemning* the same Things; than which, nothing more severe could be imposed by the greatest Tyrant, and greatest Foe. 'Tis not in vigorous Health, boundless Fortune, unrestrained Liberty, or that Liberty improv'd by Skill, and Experience into an *Art of Debauchery*,

bauchery, to give him Satisfaction, nay, *not* to give him Inquietude, though *Virtue*, though *Reason* did not interpose: The *Body* only would find out the Vanity, the Te-deum, the bad Effect of Voluptuousness, and bare *Instinct* would reproach him with it. His *past* gives Regret, his *present* dissatisfies, and his *future* deceives: His *Imagination* imposes on his *Senses*; his *Senses* weaken, and vex his *Understanding*; and his Understanding censures them *both: They* persist, *That* grows peevish, and impotent. Thus the divided Man, like a divided Family, is the Seat of Misery, and Object of Contempt.

WITH regard to the chief Branch of Sensuality, and its fatal Consequences, it may be truly said, that nothing is more stinging than a bad *Woman*'s *Hatred*, except her *Caresses*; nothing is more to be declin'd than her *Deformity*, except her *Charms*. But as for a Good Woman, *Her Price is beyond Gold. She is a Pillar of Rest.*

THE *Man of Pleasure*, as the Phrase is, is the most ridiculous of all Beings: He travels, indeed, with his Ribbon, Plume, and Bells; his *Dress*, and his *Musick*, but through a Toilsome, and Beaten Road; and every day nauseously repeats the same Tract. Throw an Eye into the gay World, what see we, for the most part, but a set of Querulous, Emaciated, Fluttering, Phantastical

A true Estimate of Human Life. 53

stical Beings, worn out in the keen Pursuit of Pleasure; Creatures that *know, own, condemn, deplore,* yet still *pursue* their own Infelicity? The decay'd *Monuments* of Error! The thin *Remains* of what is called Delight!

IN a Word, to suppose *Sense alone* can make a Man happy, is to suppose *Reason* superfluous, which is blasphemous, and absurd: But sensuality brings such a Grossness on the Understanding, that this Argument will not be so much as *comprehended* by those who have the greatest Need of being *affected* by it. Now the Cause of their not comprehending it, is their total Inexperience, and Ignorance of the Pleasures of *Reason:* Which Ignorance proves this gay, this gallant Creature, this *Patron* of Pleasures, and *Professor* of Delight, (what he little suspects) in Reality, the greatest *Niggard* in Enjoyment, the greatest *Self-denier* in the World.

SECONDLY, *Ambition.* Voluptuousness has its Intervals: When *Sense* is satisfied, it pauses for the Revival of its Flame; like *Eruptions,* it rages, and rests by Turns: But Ambition, like a *Conflagration,* burns on incessant; the more it has, the more it craves; the more it devours, the stronger is its Fury. *Success* but sets it new Tasks, and is as severe to the Ambitious, as *Misfortune* to other Men. Every Difficulty

Difficulty he cuts off, seven rise in its Stead: so that the *Character* of the most ambitious Man that ever liv'd, is a proper *Motto* for all his Sons, whose Sport, like the *Leviathan*'s, makes a Tempest, and is the Ruin of all about them. *Nil actum reputans, dum quid superesset agendum.* That is, It is their Maxim, *To know no Rest.* How differs then *Ambition* from *Slavery?* As severe *Exercise* from hard *Labour;* The Thing is the same, only *here* it is Necessity, and *there* it is Choice; that is, *there,* it is *Wretchedness,* and *Folly* too.

THE *Ambitious* thinks all Happiness is deriv'd from *Comparison,* and that Highest, and Happiest is the same Thing: Nor knows that to be *high,* is not always to be *happy;* but to be *happy,* is always, and truly to be *high.* If his Notion is right, how have the Wisest of all Ages, and all Nations been mistaken? Either they have persever'd in an eternal, and obstinate Error, in asserting *Content* to be Happiness, or he is not happy at all; for Ambition imports an Absence, nay, a Disdain of *Content:* And indeed it has the Glory, if 'tis a Glory, of being far from it. Disappointment in small Things, gives the Ambitious no small Anxiety; Success in great, no great Satisfaction, because there remain still greater Things than These; and while his Heart burns at some mighty Point in View, it robs him

him of the Relish of those considerable Enjoyments which Nature indulges to the meanest of her Children. The *Spring* has no *Beauty*, the *Autumn* has no *Taste*; much less has *Wisdom*, or *Religion*. He is not altogether incapable of Repenting of Religion, and thinking his Prayers a Loss of Time. Too just, I fear, is this Observation, which makes a Passage in *Aristotle* extreamly remarkable, who recounting the Vices incident to the great Men of his Age, says, " *Indevotion* was not one of them, " but that they were addicted to the Wor- " ship of the Gods, on account of the Riches " which they had receiv'd from them." But to return, The Violence of the ambitious Man's Desires sets him at a Distance from himself; he is never at Home to the present Hour, but reaching, and gasping at Joys to come; all in Possession is contemptible. To what amounts then his violent Affection for those Objects he pursues? To a strenuous Endeavour, by making them his *own*, to render them *contemptible* as fast as he can; that is, He seeks at once to *gain* a Blessing, and to *destroy* it: Nor in this only does the Ambitious appear to thwart his own Purposes, as will appear immediately.

BUT First, let us observe that he cannot be extreamly happy in the *very Exercise* of his Dominion, that fullest Gust of all his Desires;

fires; when he ſtands ſurrounded with many Circles of expecting, anxious Beings; the whole Neſt gaping-wide, while he can allay the Cravings but of Few. He has not Morſels for them all. If he has any Humanity, it muſt touch it, to ſee himſelf beſieg'd with eager Viſages, ſecret Pains, repining Hearts, diſappointed Hopes, that will ſtrike deep into the Peace of Families, and carry Diſtreſs beyond his *Knowledge*, and *perhaps* beyond his *Conception* of it. Or if theſe Stings of his Fellow-Creatures touch him not, He is ſtill *more* to be pity'd.

SEEK not of the Lord Preheminence, neither of the King in the Seat of Honour. But call in the Waves of thy Deſire, climbing over one another for ever; bid thy proud Heart be ſtill, and ſay to it, Hitherto ſhalt Thou go, and no farther: And let it, at leaſt, have the *bounds* of the Ocean, as well as the *tumult* of it.

AMONG *Ambition's Temporal* Evils (for of thoſe only I ſpeak) muſt be number'd the Terribleneſs of its Fall, which the Scripture ſets in the ſtrongeſt Light. It ſhews it in a Flame of Eloquence: In its Stile of Denunciation againſt it, It ſhakes Heaven, Earth, and Hell, and ſhall it not ſhake the Heart of Man? Give me Leave to ſet down at large, One remarkable Inſtance of *This*, collected from the Scriptures.

I

I SHALL place the *Woe of Babylon* in this Order. God's *Threatning*, His *Word of Command*, The *Execution*, The *Reflection*, The *Consequence*, The *Triumph*.

"O EARTH! Earth! hear *The Threatning,*
" the Word of the Lord, who is *or Alarm.*
" cloathed in a Vesture dip'd in Blood, and
" out of his Mouth goeth a sharp two-edged
" Sword, and his Countenance shineth as the
" Sun in his Strength. Put your selves in
" Array against *Babylon*, round about: O
" Thou *most Proud!* behold I am against
" Thee. Thou hast harden'd thy Heart in
" Pride. Thou hast provoked the Eyes of
" my Glory. Though Thou shouldst mount
" up to Heaven, and fortify the Height of
" thy Strength; Though thou shouldst exalt
" thy self as an Eagle, and build thy Nest a-
" mong the Stars, I will bring Thee down.
" O how Lofty are thy Eyes? O Thou who
" dwellest on many Waters! Abundant in
" Treasure! Thy End is come. There shall
" be *Time* no longer with Thee. I have the
" Keys of *Hell*, and of *Death*. Though
" Thou art a Fair Cedar of *Lebanon*, Though
" the Fowls of Heaven make their Nest in thy
" Boughs, and under thy Shadow dwell all
" great Nations, and thy Roots drink many
" Rivers, and all the Trees of the Garden of
" God envy the Multitude of thy Branches,
" Thou shalt be but a fading Flower. I will
" tread

"tread the Winepress of the Fierceness, and
"Wrath of Almighty God. Wherefore
"Gloriest Thou thy self in thy Vallies, thy
"flowing Vallies, Thou back-sliding Daugh-
"ter? Though thou fillest the Face of the
"World with Cities, though Thou cloathest
"they self with Crimson, and deckest Thee
"with Ornaments of Gold, and thy Face with
"Painting; in vain Thou makest thy self
"Fair, thy *Lovers* shall seek thy Life. The
"*Ambassadors of Peace shall weep bitterly.*
"Woe to the Multitude that makes a Noise,
"like the Noise of the Seas, and to the Rush-
"ing of Nations, like the Rushing of many
"Waters. I will cause the Arrogancy of the
"Proud to cease, and lay low the Haughti-
"ness of the Terrible. Though thou art as a
"Young Lion of the Nations, and as a Whale
"in the Seas, They shall bring Thee up in
"my Net. They shall set Thee a Bed in
"the midst of the Slain; thy Graves shall be
"round about Thee: Because thy Children are
"grown fat, as Heifers at Grass, and bellow
"as Bulls. I will set my Terrors in Array
"against Thee, the Arrows of the Almighty
"shall be in Thee, They shall drink up thy
"Spirits. Though all People, Nations, and
"Languages tremble before Thee, I will
"smite the Bow from thy Left-Hand, and the
"Arrows from thy Right. Give Wings to
"*Babylon* that she may fly: In vain! the
"*Lame* shall take the Prey. I will lay thy
"Flesh upon the Mountains, and fill the Val-
"lies

"lies with thy Height. I will water with
"Blood the Land wherein thou swimest, the
"Rivers shall be *full* of Thee. The Beasts
"of the Field, and the feather'd Fowl shall
"assemble to the Sacrifice on the Mountain;
"They shall eat the Flesh, and drink the
"Blood of Princes; They shall be fill'd at
"my Table with Horses, and Chariots, and
"mighty Men of War. Tho' Thou diggest
"into Hell, my Hand shall take Thee Thence;
"Though thou climbest up to Heaven, Thence
"will I bring Thee down; Though Thou
"hidest in the bottom of the Sea, I will com-
"mand my Serpent to bite Thee, *there*. I
"will send up many Hunters against Thee,
"and they shall pursue Thee from Hill to
"Hill, from Mountain to Mountain, They
"shall roll Thee down the Rocks. Thou
"shalt not lift thy self up in thy Brigandine,
"thy Tackling shall be loosed; Thou shalt
"not strengthen the Mast, nor spread the Sail;
"There is a Cry in the Ships, Though thy
"Shipboard is the Fir Tree of *Senir*, and thy
"Mast the Cedar of *Lebanon*, thine Oars the
"Oak of *Bashan*, and though the *Ashurites*
"have made thy Benches of Ivory; thy Sail fine
"Linnen with broidered Work from *Ægypt*,
"Blue, and Purple from the Isles of *Elishah*;
"*Zidon*, and *Arvad* thy Mariners, and thy
"Pilots *wise* men. Wilt Thou say before him
"that slayeth Thee, *I am a God?* And when
"in the Fire of my Wrath I put Thee out,
"I will cover the Heavens, and make the
"Stars

" Stars dark; the Moon shall be confounded,
" and the Sun ashamed; I will shake the Fir-
" mament, and the Earth shall be moved out
" of her Place; Hell from beneath shall be
" moved for Thee, to meet thy coming; It
" shall stir up the Dead, the chief ones of
" the Earth; and raise from their Thrones all
" the Kings of the Nations. The whole
" Creation shall groan! Thy Stars shall fall
" down round about Thee, and be stamped
" on the Earth.

The Words of Command " THE Lord maketh his Arm
" bare, he hath open'd his Armoury,
" and brought forth the Weapons of his Indig-
" nation; his glittering Spear, and his Shield,
" and his Chariots, from between two Moun-
" tains, two Mountains of Brass. The Pesti-
" lence goeth before Him, and behind Him a
" flaming Fire. He cometh up like a Lion
" from the swelling of *Jordan*; In the Glory
" of his Majesty He ariseth to shake terribly
" the Earth. The Lord mustereth the Host
" to Battle. Lift ye up a Banner on the High
" Mountain! Exalt the Voice! Shake the
" Hand! Harness the Horses! Get up the
" Horsemen! Stand forth with the Helmet!
" Put on the Brigandines! Prepare Thee!
" Stand fast! Go up O *Elam*! Besiege O *Me-*
" *dia*! Ye Kingdoms of *Ararat*! *Minni*!
" and *Ashchenaz*! Ye are my Battle Axe.
" Come up ye Horses! and rage ye Chariots!
" and let the Mighty Men come forth. Make
           " bright

A true Estimate of Human Life. 61

"bright the Arrows! and gather the Shields!
"Arise ye Princes! and anoint the Buckler!
"Set up a Standard on the Walls! Make the
"Watch Strong! Prepare the Ambush! Cast
"up a Bank! Call the Archers! Spare no Ar-
"rows! Set the Engines of War against her
"Wall! With Axes break down her Tow-
"ers! Burst her Bars! her Pillars of Iron, and
"her Walls of Brass! A Sword! a Sword is
"sharpen'd! Ah! It is made bright! It is
"wrap'd up for the Slaughter. Their Horses
"Hoofs are like Flint; and their Wheels like
"a Whirlwind. Their Arrows are sharp,
"their Bows bent; the Quiver rattles against
"Thee. The Valleys are full of Chariots,
"the Horsemen set themselves in Array at the
"Entering of the Gates. The snorting of
"the Horses is heard from *Media*; the whole
"Land trembles at the Neighing of the
"Strong. Nations lift up a Shout against
"Her, They set their Thrones before Her
"Gates. They roar like a Lion, like a
"young Lion; They roar like the Roaring
"of the Sea. No Man shall spare his Bro-
"ther. Cursed is He who keepeth back his
"Sword from Blood.

"Lo! the Shield of the Mighty *The Execution.*
"is made red; the Valiant are in
"Scarlet. The Chariots are with flaming
"Torches; The Fir Trees are terribly
"shaken. They rage in the Streets, they
"justle one another in the broad Ways,
"They

"They run like Lightnings, the Prancing
"Horses! and jumping Chariots! The
"Horse is struck with Astonishment; and
"the Rider with Madness. A Day of
"Wrath, and Distress; of Desolation, and
"Darkness; of the Trumpet, and Alarm!
"All Hands are faint; and every Heart
"melts. Their Children are dash'd to
"pieces before their Eyes; their Houses
"spoil'd; their Wives ravish'd; their Wo-
"men with Child are rip'd up. The Blood
"of the Souls of the Innocents is upon them.
"Watchman! What of the Night! Watch-
"man! What of the Night? Enquire! Re-
"turn! Come! One Post runs to meet a-
"nother, and one Messenger to meet another
"to tell the King of *Babylon* that his City
"is taken at one End; That the Passages
"are stop'd, the Reeds burnt with Fire,
"the Men of War affrighted. They scale
"the Wall, they climb the Houses, Death
"comes in at his Windows, like a Thief.
"The Gates of the Rivers are open'd; the
"Palace is dissolv'd. Pangs take hold on
"them, as on a Woman in Travel. They
"are amaz'd; Their Faces are as Flames.
"They are fed with their own Flesh; and
"Drunken with their own Blood; as with
"sweet Wine. Howl O Gate! Cry O City!
"*Bell* boweth down! *Nebo* stoopeth! *Me-
"rodack* is confounded! They stoop, they
"bow down together. Thou saidst, I shall
"sit a Lady for ever, I shall not be a
"Widow. Lo! Thy Sons have fainted,
"they

" they lie at the Heads of all the Streets,
" like a wild Bull in a Net; They are full
" of the Fury of the Lord. The Sword de-
" vours, it is satiate, it is drunk with Blood.
" At the Stamping of the Hoofs of the
" strong Horses, at the Rushing of the
" Chariots, and the Rumbling of the Wheels,
" the *Fathers* look not back for their *Chil-*
" *dren*. The Mighty stumbleth against the
" Mighty, and both fall together. They
" roar as Lyons, and yell as Lyon's Whelps.
" Her broad Walls are utterly broken, her
" high Gates are burn'd with Fire; In Fire
" her People labour; and labour in vain!
" Her Mighty Men are taken, their Bows
" are broken; I have made her Princes,
" her Wise, and her Mighty drunk with
" the Cup of Trembling. They sleep a
" Perpetual Sleep. O Thou Sword of the
" Lord! How long will it be before Thou
" art Quiet? Put up Thy self in the Scab-
" bard; Rest, and be still.

" MY Sword is fill'd with *The Reflection.*
" Blood; It is Fat; It is bath'd
" in Heaven. With the Sole of my Feet
" have I dry'd up all the Waters of besieg'd
" Places. How the Hammer of the whole
" Earth is broken? *Babylon* is Fallen! is
" Fallen! She that was great among the
" Nations, and Princess among the Pro-
" vinces! The Glory of Dominion! The
" Beauty of the *Chaldee*'s Excellency! The
" Golden

"Golden City, that went out by Thou-
"sands! The Crown of Pride! Alas! alas!
"That mighty City, That was cloath'd
"with fine Linnen, Purple, and Scarlet;
"and deck'd with Gold, Precious Stones,
"and Pearls! She who was call'd the Lady
"of Kingdoms; That Crowning City,
"whose Merchants were Princes, and her
"Traffickers the Honourable of the Earth.
"That was as a Golden Cup in the Hand
"of the Lord, with which He made drunk
"the Princes of the Earth, and the Nations
"Mad. Thy Pomp, and the Sound of thy
"Viol is brought down to the Grave; the
"Worms are spread over Thee. Thou art
"become an Astonishment, and all that
"pass by Hiss at Thee. Thy Pile is deep,
"and large, of Fire, and much Wood, and
"the Breath of the Lord like a Stream of
"Brimstone hath kindled it: The Breath
"of the Lord, whose Fire is in *Zion*, and
"his Furnace in *Jerusalem*. Thy *Tophet*
"shall not be quench'd, Night, nor Day,
"the Smoak of it shall go up for ever, and
"for ever. Wild Beasts of the Islands shall
"cry in thy desolate Houses, and doleful
"Creatures in thy pleasant Palaces; Satyrs
"shall dance there, they shall cry to their
"Fellows. It shall be an Habitation of
"Dragons, and the Court of Owls. A
"Wolf of the Evening shall spoil Thee;
"and a Leopard shall watch over thy City.

"THY

"THY King spake, and said: Is this not great *Babylon* which I have built, for the House of the Kingdom, by the Might of my Power, and for the Honour of my Majesty? I will ascend into Heaven; I will exalt my Throne above the Stars of God; I will be like the most High. How art Thou fall'n from Heaven O *Lucifer!* Son of the Morning! Is this he that weaken'd the Nations, destroy'd Cities, held Princes Prisoners, shook Kingdoms, made the Earth tremble, and the World a Wilderness?

"THOU art cast out of thy very Grave. Thy Bones shall be spread before the Sun, and the Moon, the Queen of Heaven, which Thou lovedst; and before all the Host of Heaven which Thou worshipedst. Thy Name, Remnant, Son, and Nephew, are cut off. Thy Voice shall come out of the Ground, like the Voice of one that has a Familiar Spirit; and shall whisper out of the Dust. Thy Sons are gone down to Hell with their Weapons of War; They have laid their Swords under their Heads; but their Iniquity shall be upon their Bones, tho' they were the Terror of the Mighty in the Land of the Living.

The Consequence.

The Triumph. "A MIGHTY Angel took a Stone, like a great Mill-Stone, and threw it into the Sea, saying, Thus shall the Great *Babylon* be thrown down with Violence, and shall be found no more for ever. O ye Heavens be Astonish'd at This! Sing O ye Heavens! for the Lord hath done it: Let the Morning Stars sing together; and All the Sons of God shout for Joy. Allelujah! Allelujah! In a Voice, as of a great Multitude, as of many Waters, as of Mighty Thunderings, Allelujah! Amen, Allelujah! The Lord God Omnipotent Reigneth *."

LET no Man imagine (as some seem to do) that the *Excellency of his Understanding* hinders him from believing a *Revelation,* if He finds not something beyond all *Human* Composition, in This. What Fire, what Rapidity, what Elevation, what Enthusiasm, what Picture, what Propriety, what

---

* Though a shorter Quotation would have satisfied my present Purpose, yet since I design'd *This,* likewise, as a Specimen of a Work that endeavours to shew, in a manner yet unattempted, the Genius, and Eloquence, of the *Psalms, Prophets,* and *Job,* superiour to That of all Other Authors, I hope the Length will be excused. Prejudice on one Hand, and *implicite Admiration, and Extasy* on the Other, have left Room, and Occasion of farther Adjusting the Degree of Estimation due to these Compositions, as Compositions; some Parts of which have reach'd such a Height of Perfection, that Human Nature has not Ideas to carry her to a Conception of any thing beyond it. Two Instances of this Truth among many, are, I think, the six last Chapters of *Job,* and *Psalm* the 104th.

Opu-

Opulence, what Fancy, what Energy, what † *non Imitabile Fulmen*, is Here? How Arouzing, how Divine, but how *Terrifying* too, is This? And its sacred Inspirer forbid, that the *Ambitious* should read it for their *Pleasure* only. The Fall of Ambition is not only Possible, but Probable; nay, the Wisest of Men says, *He that exalteth his Gate* seeketh his *Fall*. And an Author of great Name, when he is prescribing Rules for the Ambitious, says, That the best Rule that can be given them, is, to prepare for a Change of Fortune. *Nebuchadnezzar, Julius, Sejanus, Woolsey*, are only leading Instances of fallen Stars; Countless Multitudes have been involv'd in the like Calamity, from the same Cause, and fill up the Terror of These notorious Warnings to the Pride of Man.

ON what did *Nebuchadnezzar*, on what does any of his Successors in Ambition set their Hearts? On *Little Things*. Let any one remove his Eye from the most Magnificent Parade, or Triumph, to the Expanse of Heaven; and instantly, what was Great is Little, what was Publick, is Private. The Trumpet, the Plume, all that can enter at *Sense* on the Face of the Earth, seems Annihilated; and to dwell on it, seems creeping into a By-Path, a *digression* from the Grandeur of our Nature, and the true

† Virg.

Majesty of Life. Let not this be thought extravagant, it is strictly just. And perhaps the best Reason why a great Part of the Creation which seems of little or no Influence to our Well-being, is notwithstanding within the Compass of our Observation, is, That it should lift the Thought, expand the Soul, Disparage the Littleness of Things below, and inflame us with Reflections of a simular Nature to This.

BUT to come close to the Point. What does the Ambitious Man aim at? At Dominion, Principality, and Power; at governing Nations, and making his Name great in the Earth. And who but the Pusilanimous, and Base, shall censure him for *this*? Whatever his Errors are, does he not shew, at least, a *Grandeur of Deportment*, and a *Magnanimity of Heart*? Neither, but altogether the Reverse.

FOR, first, As to *Magnanimity*. There is a Meanness of Spirit in passionately desiring Those Things, the *Contempt* of which requires a greater Effort of Mind, (that is a greater Magnanimity,) and bestows a fuller Happiness, than the *Possession* of them. *Magnanimity* is a Resolution able to comply with the Dictates of Reason when most difficult; if therefore Ambition is unreasonable, (as I have shewn) it must be Pusilanimous. I will not therefore call the Ambitious an *Unhappy*,

Unhappy, or a *Guilty*, (as I might) but what will touch him nearer, I will call him a *Little* Man; and if That does touch him nearer, It will be a new Argument to prove that I call him *so* with the greatest Truth.

AS to the second, *The Grandeur of his Deportment.* That is, his Distance from Subjection, and Servility. What then if it should appear that no Man is so much a Slave? Dominion over Others is indeed his Aim; but by that very Aim he most effectually subjects himself to them. Every one that can retard, or promote his Purposes, has an Awe over him; Is the Object of his anxious Application, and servile Fear; Disciplines his Deportment, and pains his Mind. *Not to expect* is the only Means to be Free, and He is all Expectation, that is, all Slavery; *while Dominion*, nay *because* Dominion is his only Aim. And thus it fares with all irregular Pursuits of Happiness; They contradict the Purpose of God, and therefore must counter-act themselves; for God will not be controul'd. He has assign'd *other* means of Happiness, and to convince us of it most strongly, they that make not use of *his* Means, but their *own* to that end, shall not only fail of it, but their Endeavours shall be their Hindrance, shall work them backwards, and set them at a greater Distance from it. Thus the *Voluptuary* just mentioned, while he too warmly pursues

the

the *Objects*, most effectually blunts the *Powers* of Appetite. The *Covetous*, while He inordinately desires to become Rich, though he succeeds in all his Attempts, he fails of his End; nay fails of it *by* that Success; God to chastise, and as it were, to insult him too, gives him the *Thing*, but witholds the Enjoyment; nay commands *Abundance* to make him *Poor*. Thus, and thus only can that miraculous Conduct of the Covetous be accounted for, of whom

THIRDLY, I am about to speak. The Covetous strongly exposes Human Nature by shewing us an Instance in *one* Person, how much She *desires*, and how little She *wants*. For who subsists on so Little, who grasps at so much? He mistakes the *Means* for the *End*; *Money* for *Enjoyment*; Nay the means, in his Hands, makes *against* his End, and the *Power* of *Enjoying* is an *Inducement* to *Self-denial*. The Gold that comes into his Possession but *changes* its *Mine*, and is farther from the Light than ever. His *Impiety*, and his *Folly* are equally gross. As to the *First*, He is often in Scripture call'd an Idolater, because he Worships his Wealth: As to the *Second*, That his Idol, like other Idols of Old, requires severer Service of him than the *true* God; more rigid Austerities than Religion enjoins; His Toils, his Self-denials, his fervent Devotion to *Gain*, is Greater than That which might carry him to *Heaven*. Covetousness is nothing but the

Painful

A true Estimate of Human Life. 71

Painful *art* of making Industry Sinful, Wealth Indigent, Influence Dishonourable, Life Sordid, Death Terrible, and Heirs Ungrateful without any manner of Guilt.

BUT to set it in the clearest and shortest Light; What is Wealth? a *Security* put into our Hands, That the Enjoyments of this World shall be delivered to us whenever we please, on *that* Title. Now if that Title rather Denies, than Gives us those Enjoyments, It loses its Nature; It is no longer a *Title* indulg'd to our Necessities, but it is a *Warrant* served on our Folly, to deliver us over to Wretchedness, to Shame, and to Want. So that the Miser has no *Wealth*.

NOTHING is so strange as Man's inextinguishable Thirst for *More*; Nay, he pants after That which he *has*. For I affirm that infinite Numbers have *sufficient* Means of Happiness already in their Hands, and *sufficient* Means is what they are reaching after; For who needs more? But Men *know not* what they possess. How Few have made an Inventory of their own Blessings? How few know what they do *not* want? Hence, *Know thy self* was said to come from Heaven: For, without it, no Man can be Content. Our Pains are from our *Desires*, not from our *Wants*. For which most material Truth I shall mention Two Arguments.

FIRST, If we Examine, we shall often find, that after burning with some vehement Desire,

Desire, we are Quieted by *Despair*, as *much*, and perhaps, *more happily*, than we should have been by *Success*.

SECOND, Let some great Pain seize us in our most rapid Pursuit after what we imagine Essential to our Peace, and the ceasing of that *superior Pain* will give us a *momentary* Conviction, that we were *really*, then, Happy, when we *thought* our selves Miserable. But Folly soon reclaims us as her own.

IF we could lay aside but Two Things, First, Our *own Imagination*, which makes us think Things Necessary which are not; Secondly, Our Deference for the *Opinion of the World*, which makes us Incapable of being Happy, unless we are *Thought* so, the Majority of Mankind would be much Happier than they, at present, imagine; They would grow Rich *extempore*, and be more Indebted to the Removal of an Error in Judgment, than to any *possible* Success they could have in their Pursuits of Wealth. Our Error in the present Case (as in most Others) proceeds from *partial Views*, from not taking in the *Whole*. We look only on those *Above us*, which strains our Hearts in Pursuit, and puts all our Faculties painfully on the Stretch; Whereas if we look'd on those *below* us too; It would abate our Ferment, Remit our painful Intention, and inspire quite *new* Sentiments of our own State. Now on our Sentiments (which Few observe) our Happiness depends. It lies in in Thoughts, and not in Things. Things are *opaque* Bodies, which have no Light of their own, and are only capable of reflecting to Advantage the Gayety beaming on them from our own Hearts. Hence, the very Unhappy fly Publick, and Pompous Scenes of Life; becaufe, while Gay to *others*, they are Dark to *them*, and therefore, more provokingly fo, than *Retreat*. It is not the Man's Bufinefs, who defires Happinefs, to increafe his *riches*, but to give his *underftanding* fo juft a Judgment of Things, and his *affections* fo rational a Temper, that He could *not* be more Happy, though he *were* more Rich. Nay fome have parted with their Riches for the fake of Happinefs. But, *in this*, the Faith of Annals, in the Mifer's opinion, will *labour* very much.

THE Foundation of Error in this Point, is, all our Pains, and Pleafures, are from *Senfe*, or *Imagination*, and not from *Reafon*. Now Content is an *Art*; I have *Learn'd* to be Content, fays the Apoftle. Neither Nature, nor Chance, nor Circumftances can give it. The whole Body of Pagan, and Chriftian Ethicks are the Rules of this Art. Now the Mifer profeffes an Art directly the Reverfe of it. *He* is Wife, (which is another Word for *Happy* in this Cafe,) who can fay I have not Much, but no Man has More, for I have all I want. *Socrates* faid with Wit, but with Judgment too. " He that need *Leaft*, is moft like the " Gods, who need *Nothing*.

L.   FOURTHLY,

FOURTHLY, I am to speak of the *Vain*. This is the most Distinguish'd Son of Folly, and has the most airy Happiness of them all. His Brothers beforementioned, though themselves to be laugh'd at, laugh at Him. He seeks his Felicity entirely in the Opinions of *others*, and but rarely finds it there; for the World, by his very Name, has pronounc'd against him; from the Emptiness of his Pursuit, and the Thinness of his Enjoyment, is he call'd *Vain*. The Former *Wish* at least for something Substantial, but His very *Wish* is a *Reproach*.

AS the too Modest is pain'd by being *in* the Publick Eye, He is pain'd by being *out* of it. What a vast Expence is He at to buy Spectators? For to what other End is his splendid Person, and Equipage, his large Parks, Palaces, Rivers, and Cascades? How Expensive? and how Useless? *Sense* is too Narrow, it wants Compass to take them in; Less Things would gratify *That* more. The *Understanding* condemns them; Childish *Imagination* only approves, and that too but for a Moment; What are these Pageantries, but *Larger Toys* with which it Plays a-while, and then grows weary of them? What are they, but huge Monuments of Mistake, Subjects for Popular Talk, and an Immense Tax paid for *Rumour*, for sure it cannot be call'd *Fame*?

HOW He Gazes on, and Touches, and Retouches, and as it were sollicits his shining Ornaments

Ornaments to give him some extraordinary Sensation, somewhat adequate to the Desire he indulg'd *for*, or the Expectation he entertained *from* them? but in Vain. They were much more Powerful in *Idea*, than they are in *Fact*. It is falling in Love with our own Mistaken Ideas that makes Fools, and Beggars of half Mankind.

THE *Vain* is a Beggar of Admiration. Begging is an unreputable Profession; but as we are Dependent Beings, we must all be Beggars in some Degree. The Scandal therefore of this Practise depends on two Things, the Character of the Person *from whom*, and the Value of the Things *which* we beg. Now the Vain begs from all, even the *most Ignoble*; and He begs *Nothing*; I mean, what turns to no Account. He is more Noble that asks *Bread*, than He who asks a Bow, or the Glance of an Eye; for *that* is more worth.

IN what does this Man lay out the Faculties of an Immortal Soul? That Time, on which depends Eternity? That Estate, which well dispos'd of, might in some measure, purchase Heaven? What is his serious Labour, subtle Machination, ardent Desire, and reigning Ambition? — *to be seen.* This Ridiculous, but *true* Answer, renders all grave Censure almost Superfluous. If the World was fill'd with such as These, all Arts, and Engines of Discipline, and of Death, for chastisement of Offence, might seem needless; let the Law they violate, or the Power they offend, but condemn them to *Retreat*.

BUT to come close to the Point. What is it the *Vain* would have? He would be Admired; He begs an *alms* of Admiration from every Passer by, and his Happiness *starves* without it. Now what does This Desire imply? It implies that he cannot be Happy without their Leave. Thus is He by *choice* the most Precarious Creature on Earth. The most Precarious Creature is the most wretched, and, therefore, the most Precarious by *choice*, is the most Foolish too; If any will deny that the most Precarious Being is most wretched, let them consider that the Reverse, the least Precarious Being, is the most Happy, for That is God: and the farther we are remov'd from Independency, and Self-sufficiency, the farther are we remov'd from that Standard of Wisdom, and Happiness.

I SHALL dismiss the *Vain* with one Observation more. We ought *particularly* to guard against This Folly, for a Reason very *particular* too. Other Vices are promoted by Vices, but This is often Nourish'd by *Virtue* itself.

THUS have I, I think, prov'd, That The *Voluptuous* is the Greatest *Self-denier*; That the *Ambitious* is the Greatest *Slave*; That the *Covetous* has no Wealth; and That the Vain whose Idol is *Admiration*, is the Greatest Object of *Contempt*.

THE

THE Considerations which have been alledg'd to the Discredit of Human Happiness have been, *hitherto*, drawn from General Topicks; *One* remains, That is *too Peculiar*. We have lately lost our King; That sad Occasion first suggested *This Subject* to me, which, now, It supports with an unwelcome Argument; for when our Sovereign fell, Nature her self emphatically proclaim'd "That all "below is Vain". Too powerful a Supplement to this Discourse!

WHO, then, art Thou who settest thine Affections on Things below? Art Thou Greater than the Deceas'd? Dost Thou value thy self on thy *Birth?* The most Highly-descended is no more. Dost Thou value thy self on thy *Riches?* The King of *Britain* is no more. Dost Thou value thy self on thy *Power?* The Master of the Seas, the Arbiter of *Europe* is no more. Dost Thou glory in thy Constancy, Humanity, Affection to thy Friends, or *Encouragement of Arts?* — But I forbear. It is *Ambition* to be *Grateful*, when Princes bestow.

HOW lately were the Eyes of all *Europe* thrown on this Great Man? For *Man* let me call him, now, nor contradict the Declaration which his Mortality has made. They that find Him, now, must *seek* for Him; and seek for Him in the *Dust*. What on Earth but must tell us This World is vain, if Thrones
declare

declare it? If Kings, if *British* Kings are Demonstrations of it? O Majesty! Thy *Serene Evening* indeed is, clos'd; but, Then, Thou shinest on us in thy *Meridian* Glory.

I SHALL offer one Observation on the Death of Princes, which is full to my present Purpose. A Throne is the shining Period, the golden Termination of the Worldly Man's Prospect; *his* Passions affect, *his* Understanding conceives; nothing beyond it, or the Favours it can bestow. The Sun, the Expanse of Heaven, or what lies Higher, have no Lustre in *his* Sight, no Room in his pre-engag'd Imagination, it is all a superfluous Waste. When therefore his Monarch dies, He is left in Darkness, *his* Sun is set, it is the Night of Ambition with him. Which naturally damps him into Reflection, and fills that Reflection with awful Thoughts.

WITH Reverence, then, be it spoken, what can God, in his Ordinary Means, do more, to turn his Affections into their right Channel, and send them forward to their proper End? Providence, by his King's decease, takes away the very Ground on which his Delusion rose; It sinks before him; his *Error* is supplanted, nor has his *Folly* whereon to stand; but must return, like the Dove in the Deluge, to his own Bosom again.

BY *This*, is he convinc'd that his ultimate Point of View is not only Vain in its Nature, but

but Vain in Fact; It not only *may*, but *has* actually fail'd. What, then, is He under a Necessity of doing, this Boundary of his Sight remov'd? Either he must look forward, (and what is beyond it, but God?) Or, he must close his Eyes in wilful Darkness, and still repose his Trust in Things which he has *experienc'd* to be Vain. Such Accidents, therefore, however Fatal to his *Secular*, are the Mercy of God, as to his *Eternal* Interest; and say with my Text, *Set your Affections on Things above, and not on Things on the Earth.*

LET us, now, from the Throne look back, (as from an Eminence,) on the former part of our *Journey*; We have passed the several *Orders, Ages, Aims, Relations, Constitutions, Tempers, Passions*, with the four great *Impulses* of Mankind, and have found but one Report through these several Stages of our Course; The various Witnesses concur, and bring in a full Verdict against the Happiness of Human Life. They declare that all Mankind is United by Misery, in some Degree, as by (what is less Melancholy) the *Grave*, to which it leads.

AND can this World enchant us still? And can we be born for *This?* Is This a Scene for *Reason*, that Emanation of Divity to doat one? Is This the Fortune, This the Dower to which we should wed an *Immortal Soul?* Where then is the Difference between

between *Reason*, and *Absurdity?* Between *Immortality*, and the *Beasts that perish?* Be This Their Heaven, (as properly it is,) but not their Lord's, but not Man's.

I SHALL close this Discourse with a Picture of *Life* in *Miniature*, that your Memories may carry it the better: A Picture more Melancholy, than That of This Globe e'er well clear of the *Chaos*; or labouring, afterwards, under all the Wrongs, and Disgraces, that an Universal *Deluge* could inflict.

Thoughts with Regard to the Mind. BEHOLD a World! *Where* the Inhabitants are not differenced by Happiness, and Misery; but only by the different *Degrees*, and various *Colours* of Misery Universal: *Where*, the *Memory* is clouded with black Ideas of the Past; the *Imagination* over-looks the Present; and the *Understanding*, through Mercy, is Blinded to the Future: *Where*, every *Passion* may be call'd *Legion*, for its Evils are many. *Where*, Men almost universally lay aside *Intellectual* Pleasures; are most ardent Desirers of Happiness, and yet subsist it on the most Impotent Half of their Natures. *Where*, Anxiety of Thought damps Sensual Pleasure, and sensual Pleasure increases Anxiety of Thought, and impairs our Strength to support it, too. *Where*, the Soul and Body are in perpetual Hostilities, aggrieving each other, and External

Acci-

Accidents seem superfluous to our Misery; Thus the Poor Man, like Devoted *Jerusalem*, besieg'd without, and divided within, is a Complication of Infelicity.

WHERE, *Success* must be procur'd by our Infinite Care, and *Ruin* follows on the Contrary; so that all the sad Choice indulg'd to Mankind, is, of infinite Care, or Destruction. Besides, the more we have of Credit, Wealth, or Power, the more we *may* lose; nor is any Man entirely free from the Apprehensions of it; so that our Possessions *imply*, and *provide* for our Misery. *Where*, an Independent Pleasure is very *Severe:* a Dependent, very Frail. *Where*, *Pleasure* often exacts such Hardships from her Votary, that *Austerity* cannot improve upon them. *Where*, nothing Pleases but in Prospect, and to please in Prospect only, is not to disappoint alone, but to *deride* us, too. *Where*, what *Exalts* the Spirits shortens Life by that Expence, and what *Depresses*, makes the shortest Life too Long. *Where*, Days are Long, yet Life is Short. *Where*, we stand as in a Battel, Thousands daily falling round us, and yet we forget our own Mortality; nay, are harden'd into an Insensibility of it, by these very Proofs of its Approach; and start, like *David*, when we hear, " Thou art the Man". *Where*, *Experience*, which is *truly* the Greatest Blessing of Life, is the severest Discipline

To Externals.

of it, too; and *Diverſion*, which is *ſuppos'd* a Bleſſing, only ſignifies that to our ſelves we are Inſupportable. *Where*, *Sorrow* is as the Stem, or Root of Life; *Joy* but as its Flower, expected at remote Seaſons only, Then often blighted, or if it Blooms, in Blooming dies. *Where*, all is Vexatious, or Mix'd, or Fugitive. *Where*, Pains aſſault us, Deluſions ſurround us, and Terrors hang o'er us. *Where*, we are *Reſtleſs* in Purſuit, *Diſatisfied* in Fruition, and *Perſecuted* with Remorſe. *Where*, we are ever Purſuing, and ever condemning the ſame Things; ever Accuſing *Hope* of its broken Faith, and ever Truſting on; ever gaſping after Senſual Enjoyments, and ever Impairing our Appetite for them. *Where*, Objects, as well as Appetites decay; or if they laſt, laſt not to us, through the Fickleneſs of our Choice. *Where*, we are yearly burying ſome favourite Amuſement, or Pleaſure; and They that ſucceed are leſs Exquiſite, and full as Mortal. *Where*, we ſpend moſt of our Days in climbing the Hill of our Fortune, which ſuſpends, by Labour, any ſerious Thought; and when we have climb'd it, and are about to change Toil for Enjoyment, we ſtart to ſee our Grave ſo near us on t'other Side. *Where*, Life with moſt Men is *to come*, till It is *paſt*.

To the Profeſ- *ſions, and Nature of Things.* *WHERE*, the grave *Employments* of Mankind are but ſtrenuous Follies; nor differenc'd from

A true Estimate of Human Life. 83

from those of Children, but by their Magnitude, and their Guilt. *Where,* the several Occupations of Life are but Fortifications against *Want,* and often frail ones, too. *Where,* among *Professions* are the Lawyer, and the Soldier, Professors of Quarrel and Death; Fortune, and Life their Prey. *Where,* the Infirmities of our *Bodies* demand, and support One Profession; the Infirmities of our *Mind,* Another; and the Misadventures of our *Fortune* constitute an ample Portion in the whole World of Literature. *Where,* the very *Elements* wage War against us; and have their Inundation, Shipwreck, Earthquake, Famine, Pestilence, Volcano's, and Conflagration. *Where,* we cannot make way from our Doors, but through the Cries of *Indigence,* or *Disease.* *Where,* Hospitals, and Bedlams are publick *Necessaries.* *Where,* the very *Appellations* of a large part of Mankind can't be *heard* without Compassion; *Widows!* and *Orphans! Where, Tears* are a Distinction of the whole Species from other Creatures. *Where,* Youth often languishes like a Tempest-beaten Flower, and Age shews its Injuries like a Blasted Oak.

Where, History, for the most part, is nothing but a large Field of Misfortune, and to dip into almost any Page of it, is, to dip into Blood; Into Blood, Persecutions, Inquisitions, Treasons, Assassinations, Sieges, Servitudes: Or if sometimes

To History.

a *Triumph* breaks through this general Cloud, as Lightning thro' Night, it vanishes almost as soon; and while it lasts, it is a Proof, and Memorial of Misery; For what is a *Triumph*, but the Gay Daughter of Destruction, and Death? *Where, Hardheartedness*, and *Lust*, drinking the Tears of believing Innocence, and *Self-design*, and *Treachery*, turning every Virtue of Others, to its own Interest, and the Good Man's Ruin, (which abounds in every Record) makes Peace more Cruel than War. *Where, Happiness* is such a Stranger, that for many Ages it was *Learning* to seek the True Notion of it; and it was *but Sought*; It was not *Found*, but *Reveal'd* at last. *Where*, the Pomps, and *Prancings of the Mighty*, are but the Trapings of Woe. *Where*, the most Shining, and *Envy'd* Characters have Few of them died a Natural Death; but furnish Theme of Tragedy for succeeding Generations: Strange! that the same Persons should be the Objects of our *Envy*, and *Pity* too! Strange too! that we should have Sighs sufficient for more Miseries than our own. *Where*, the most Happy would not repeat their Course; and He was justly censur'd who wept over his Army as Mortal, because not One of that Numerous Host, but might probably *wish*, before he *found* his End. *Where*, among the many Arguments for a *Future* State, the Misery of *This* has been most strongly, and universally insisted on in all Ages; which

demon-

demonstrates an acute Sense, and too ample a Conviction of it. *Where,* Crowns have been often *Abdicated*; How often, in our own Annals is the *Palace* chang'd for the *Cloyster?* *Where, Self-murder,* at certain Periods, has been a Fashion; nay very extraordinary Methods have been taken to restrain even the Tender Sex from this Horror. *Where,* Half the Travels that have been undertook, half the Designs that have been enterpriz'd, half the Volumes that have been written, have been Refuges from Uneasiness of Heart; and the *Last* are not more the Immortal Monuments of human Wit, than of human Infelicity. *Where* Happiness is an *Art,* and Content is an *Art;* what Libraries have been written to teach it? Whatever Success they have in teaching *That,* they certainly teach us *This,* That Unhappiness, and Discontent are *Natural.*

WHERE, a *Smile* is often an Ambush, as it was on the Face of *Domitian,* on which it seldom shone, but when Rancour gather'd at his Heart. *Where,* Enmity is Sincere, Friendship often a Name; and it is *Ruin* to trust Those, whom not to trust is almost a *Crime,* as a Relation, a Friend, a Brother! *Where,* many fall from Credit, Fortune, Life, with *Cæsar's* Exclamation, " *And This from Thee*"? *Where,* provoking our Foes has not ruin'd half so many, as Confiding in those of a Contrary

To Friendship.

Cha-

Character. He needs no Foe, who is entirely at the Mercy of his Friends. *Where*, more Hearts pine away in secret Anguish for Unkindness from Those who should be their Comforters, than for any other Calamity in Life. *Where*, Bills of Mortality would scarce be mournful, if Bills of private Calamity were in use. Who has not seen, who has not foreseen, nay who almost, has not felt, a Bleeding Heart? *Where*, Evil Arts usurp the Name, and Port of *Wisdom*, though scarce worthy to be call'd *Cunning*. Now Cunning is but the Top of a *Fool*'s Character, and Wisdom it self is but the Bottom, or Inferior Part of the Character of an *Honest Man*. *Nulla Bona, nisi Honesta*.

To Family-Affliction. Where the Honest, Confiding Heart takes a Virgin Flower into his Bosom, and often finds a Sting under it. *Where*, the Fond Mother, *to-Day*, looks with Transport on the Reward of her long Labour, and painful Travel, which changes perhaps, *To-Morrow*, the Cradle for the Grave. *Where*, the feeble Father follows a favourite, an only Daughter, the Delight of his Eye! the Rest of his Age! to her long Home, which He perhaps has wished for himself in vain; and sheds those Tears on her Ashes, which should express his Joy for the Happy Disposal of her in Life: Or perhaps the Case is still worse, He sees her Youth, and Beauty, and Innocence fallen into Arms, to him more Dreadful than

Those

Those of Death. *Where*, the Son of some Great House, its Hope, Joy, and Support, the Sole Heir, of Riches, Titles, and golden Schemes, falls immaturely, grasp'd by Death, as the Pillars were by *Sampson*; and the whole Structure is sorely shaken, if it does not follow on his Fall. *Where*, many a numerous Family lives, in Innocence, Peace, Plenty, Reputation, under the Wing of an indulgent, prudent, and industrious Father; the Father dies, they are scatter'd, like a Sheaf of Corn when the Band is broke, and become the prey of Guilt, Want, Anxiety, and Shame. *Where*, the Comforts of Life have their Pangs; their Jars, Jealousies, Interruptions, Decays, and Extinction. *Where*, Grudge, Animosity, and Revenge wound deep; but deeper (when They wound) Relation, Friendship, Love; for Love has its Barbarities, and frequently may be mistaken for Hatred by its Effects. There are sometimes malignant Tempers in Families; such *Domestick* Maladies are like Ulcers in the Vitals; Extremities cannot cure them, they cannot be cut off.

Mixt Thoughts. *W*HERE, the Night is an Idle Dream, and the Day little better. *Where*, every one is *Witness*, or *Patient* of Affliction; ever telling sad Tales of Others, till He becomes a Tale Himself; the Tale of a Day! and then is utterly forgotten. He *Liv'd and Dy'd*, is an Epitaph for much the Greatest part of Mankind. *Where* He that has reach'd his

his Meridian is One of a Thousand, his Friends and Relations lie dead around him; Half of his Conversation is gather'd from the Tomb. What are the Gay, Young, Beautiful, Brave, Learned, Wise, Good, in which He once perhaps was Rich, what are They? a Tear! a Sigh! *Where*, Youth has the Pain of *getting*, Age of *leaving* its Riches; *Affection* being rarely strong enough in us to make the parting with them Agreeable. *Where*, *Fears*, and *Pangs*, only give a Relish of the Contrary; and our Pleasure generally as it rises *from*, so it ends *in* them, too. *Where*, the Pain of *Impatience* turns us over to the Pain of *Satiety*, scarce divided by the *Moment* of Delight. *Where* Pain is oftner sunk by *new* Pain, than heal'd by superveening Pleasure? *Where*, Real Evils are *Frequent*; Imaginary, *Perpetual*; And the Happiest thanks some Other's Wretchedness, for putting him in mind, that He is not the most wretched Himself. *Where*, I *was* Happy, a Few may possibly say, I *shall* be Happy Most say, I *am* Happy, None: Now if None are Happy on the Present, it is a Demonstration that Happiness is absent from us All. The *Present* is All that our Parent Nature, properly, gives us; and That like peevish Children, we will not tast; Thus between the Law of our Condition, and the Perversness of our Temper, we have nothing at all; we are very Poor, Subsisting, or rather Starving our thin Happiness on Dreams, and Shadows of Good to come; perhaps, never to come; certainly,

certainly, never to come proportionate to our Conceptions of them. *Where,* Man snatches such Quick, and Terrible resentment from the smallest Occasion, that it resembles the Discharge of Ordnance at the Touch of a Reed. *Where,* to have any Chance for Happiness a Man must *Possess* the World, or *Despise* it; Now the Contempt of it, in Him that possesses it not, is a Cheat, He does *not* heartily contemn it; He mistakes his Ill-will for Contempt; and what is as Unfortunate, He that possesses it, *does* contemn it; but not from Wisdom, but Weakness, which has not the Skill to relish its Enjoyments, as they deserve. *Where, Proud Honour* stands in the Place of *Meek Religion,* Honour that disdains Compulsion, and that, consequently, must stand, or Fall, with Inclination, and Humour; He, therefore, that relies on Honour, relies on Humour, and He that relies on Humour, *is* a Fool, and *must* be a Wretch in the End. *Where,* the Two points the World's wise Man aims at, are, First to get the better of *Natural Instinct,* so as not to be betray'd by it into any Humanities, in which He does not find his own Immediate Account; Secondly, to surmount the *Prejudices, and Timorousness of Education,* to throw the Virtues, and Vices into One Heap, *like a Man;* Thence, to be drawn out, *indifferently,* as Interest directs; Interest, which is his *God,* and his *Bible,* the Custom of the World. *Where,* many Men suppose you a Knave, or conclude You a Fool; and

N   call

call you so by their Professions of disinterested Friendship; by which they only mean to steal your Affections, and the good Effects of them. *Where*, Compassion, with some, passes for Weakness, and you must suppress your Sighs, as in the Theatre, not to be laugh'd at; He is look'd on as an *Ideot*, who is not above being a *Man*. *Where*, Men seek not the *Means* of Serving, but an *excuse* for not Serving Others; and *Words* change their Nature, and do not *reveal*, but cover the Mind; the *Passions* themselves, those Betrayers of Truth, are taught to *act a Part*; the very *Eye* can lie, and that Natural *Window* of the Soul, has a Skreen before it, that you may not see through; He only, who discovers his *own Interest*, gives you a Key to his Heart: In a word, *Where*, the Honest Man (who alone is worthy of Good) if he judges of Men by himself, is Undone. *This* may be call'd Satire, but, by the same Rule, the Scripture is so too. *Where*, to dissemble Injuries, is the greatest Shock to Nature, and Shame to Honour, yet, at the same time, the greatest *Art of Life*. *Where*, He that has not learn'd the World must go out of it, or be a *Jest*, and an *Unfortunate* in it; He that has learn'd it, has learn'd it with Discipline, and by that time, he is well Master of the *Game*, his *Candle is put out*. It is Hard to learn the World, but Harder to Unlearn it; and not to Unlearn it, will, one Day, prove *more* Fatal. *Where*, we will not believe *Yesterday*, but hope favourably of *Tomorrow*;

morrow; as if then there would be a *New Sun,* a *New Nature,* a *New Self;* They *pray* for That, who almoſt *curſe* its Fellow. *Where,* Sorrow is Fruitleſs, and *Laughter is Mad. Where,* at the ſeveral *Tides* of Good Fortune, the *Head* tells the *Heart,* well, now, we are *Happy,* which the Heart ſcarce believes, or believes it *implicitly*: Whenever we ſay to our ſelves let us ſit down, and enjoy Life, we diſcover the Cheat, like One deluded by *Perſpective,* by bringing it to the Touch. *Nothing* will do; Buſineſs, conſidering *Paſſion,* and *Accident* is a Toil certainly; Idleneſs is worſe; and Books are a weak Reſourſe; A Man ſhould no more Read, than Eat, without an Appetite; if He does, the Book will be near as much Amuſed, and Edified by the Man, as He by the Book. *Where,* Multitudes, (ſtrange! and ridiculous! but for the Horror of it) complain they have nothing to do, when every *Step* is a Step toward a *Grave,* every *Minute* an Approach to an *Eternity:* Beſides, if Men well knew the Buſineſs of *this* World, and would acquit themſelves like Maſters in it, *Want* of Time would be their great Complaint. Nay he that lays down but this one ſimple Rule, That he will be in the Right whereever he is, or whatever he is about, will never have one idle Moment, tho' he has not the Important Cares of Nations, or even of Families on his Hands.

WHERE, the *Past* is a very Dream, and the *Future* a sore Travel. *Where*, the tender Mother sheds Tears over her Helpless Infant, and the Careful Father pours Groans over them Both; Groans conscious of the Present, and Presaging of the Future. *Where*, sometimes Nations groan, as One Man, under a General Calamity; Nor is the Whole Earth at all priviledg'd from the severe Condition of any one Nation of it. *Where*, Nature is perpetually pouring her Children in vast Tides out of *Time*, into *Eternity*; and the Survivers take the Evil, and refuse the Good. They are but the more Melancholy, not the Wiser for it. *Where*, we are Born with Pain, and Die with Amazement. *Where*, Life is the *Slave of Misery*, and yet (most strange, and Deplorable!) the *King of Terrors* is Death.

Sunt Lacrymæ Rerum, & mentem Mortalia tangunt.

ALMOST the whole Book of *Ecclesiastes* might be transcrib'd as a Scriptural Support of what is here said; and its Author, it is well known, received Wisdom as an immediate Gift from God, in Superiority to all the Rest of Mankind.

I SHALL conclude by saying what is most True, that Human Life is like a Dishonest Creditor, it pus off our *Youth*, and *Manhood*,

Manhood, with Lies from Day to Day, then owns the Cheat, and gives our *Age* an absolute Denial.

IF this Account is Juft, as I think it is, What is *Human Happinefs?* A Word! a Notion! a Day-dream! a Wifh! a Sigh! a Theme to be talk'd of! a Mark to be fhot at, but never Hit! A Picture in the Head, and a Pang in the Heart of Man. *Wifdom* recommends it gravely, *Learning* talks of it pompoufly; our *Underftanding* liftens to it eagerly, our *Affection* purfues it warmly, and our *Experience* defpairs of it irretrievably. *Imagination* perfuades fome that they have found it, but it is while their *Reafon* is afleep; *Pride* prevails with Others to boaft of it, but it is *only* a *Boaft*, by which they may deceive their Neighbours, but not Themfelves; *Felicity of Conftitution*, and *Suavity of Manners* make the neareft Approach to it, but it is *only* an *Approach*; *Fortune*, the *Nature of Things*, the *Infirmities of the Body*, the *Paffions of the Mind*, the *Dependence on Others* the *Prevalence of Vice*, the very *Condition of* (uncorrected) *Humanity* forbids an Embrace. Wine, Beauty, Mufick, Pomp, Study, Diverfion, Bufinefs, Wifdom, All that Sea or Land, Nature or Art, Labour or Reft can beftow, are but poor Expedients to heave off the Infupportable Load of an Hour from the Heart

The Defcription of Human Happinefs.

Heart of Man; the Load of an *Hour*, from the Heir of an *Eternity!* If the *Young*, or *Unexperienc'd*, or *Vain*, or *Profligate* only were subject to this Weakness, It were something; but when the *Learned*, and *Wise*, and *Grave*, and *Grey* — It shocks! It mortifies! and with Shame, and Pity, my Mind turns from its Purpose, and goes *backward* with Reverence to throw a Veil over the Nakedness of my *Father*. In a Word, the true Notion of *Human Happiness* explained, is it self one of the strongest Proofs of our Misery. For how can we speak more adequately of it, than by saying, It is *That* of which our *Despair* is as *Necessary*, as our *Passion* for it is *Vehement, and Inextinguishable*. Now *ardently* to *Thirst*, and *unavoidably* to *Despond*, with Regard to the same Thing, and That Thing of *Consequence Supream*, is the Consummation of Infelicity. I know but One solid *Pleasure* in Life, and that is our *Duty*; How *Miserable*, then, how Unwise, how Unpardonable are They, who make that *One* a *Pain?*

THE Purpose of this Discourse, as express'd in the Beginning of it, was to put This World in the Balance; and examine the Value of *Things on the Earth*. Now such as is Represented, not Aggravated, through the whole preceeding Discourse, *is*
the

the *General* State of Mankind: But It is a State of their *own Choice*; And It *may* be, though not wholly Revers'd, abundantly Reliev'd, exceedingly Brighten'd from the Clouds, The Thick Darkneſs that hangs upon it; as I ſhall endeavour to make manifeſt in the following Diſcourſe; and Thus *Vindicate Providence* from prevailing Imputations; and by laying the *Two Counter-parts* together, infer *A true Eſtimate of Human Life.*

F I N I S.

Juſt Publiſh'd,

FRIENDSHIP in DEATH: In Twenty LETTERS from the DEAD to the LIVING; amongſt which are the following, *viz.*

To the E. of *R*——— from Mr. ——— who had promiſed to appear to him after his Death.

To the Counteſs of ——— from her only Son, who died when he was two Years old.

To my Lord ——— from a young Lady who was in a Convent in *Florence.*

From *Ibrahim,* a Turkiſh *Baſſa,* to *Phiẓocles,* who had converted him to Chriſtianity.

To my Lord ——— from his deceas'd Wife.

To a Son, from his deceas'd Father, diſſuading him from engaging in a Duel, *&c.*

And to theſe Letters are added,

THOUGHTS on DEATH. Tranſlated from the Moral Eſſays of the *Meſſieurs* du Port Royal.

——*Curæ non ipſa in Morte relinquunt.*

Printed for T. Worrall. *Price* 1 s. 6 d. *ſtitch'd,* 2 s. *bound.*